Alice's Tea Cup

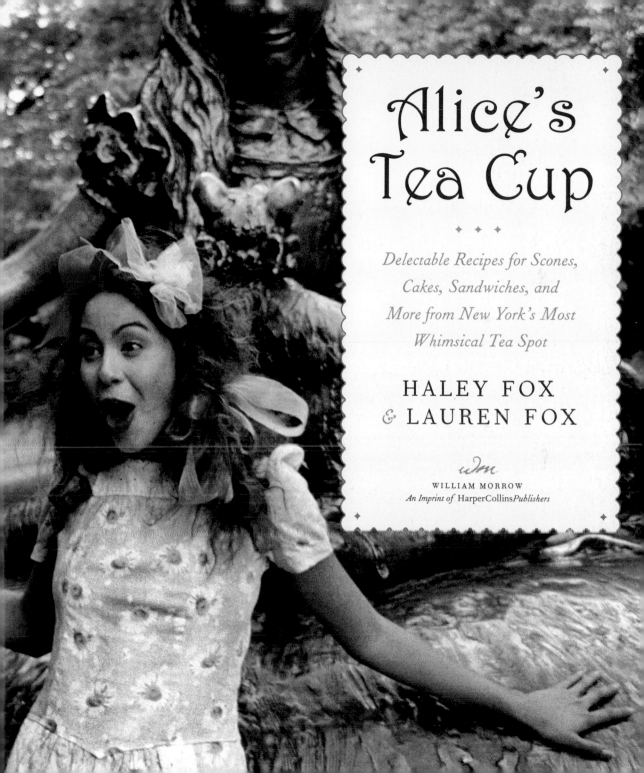

Alice's Tea Cup

*Delectable Recipes for Scones,
Cakes, Sandwiches, and
More from New York's Most
Whimsical Tea Spot*

HALEY FOX
& LAUREN FOX

WILLIAM MORROW
An Imprint of HarperCollins*Publishers*

FIRST EDITION

Designed by Joel Avirom and Jason Snyder

Library of Congress Cataloging-in-Publication Data

Fox, Haley.
   Alice's Tea Cup : delectable recipes for scones, cakes, sandwiches, and more from New York's most whimsical tea spot / Haley Fox and Lauren Fox. — 1st ed.
     p.   cm.
  Includes index.
  ISBN 978-0-06-196492-3
 1. Afternoon teas. 2. Alice's Tea Cup (Restaurant) 3. Tea. I. Fox, Lauren. II. Title.
  TX736.F685 2010
  641.5'3—dc22

2010008335

---

10 11 12 13 14 OV/RRD 10 9 8 7 6 5 4 3 2 1

*In loving memory of grandmas Fox and Thomas,
who were both sweeter than anything
we could ever bake . . .*

CONTENTS

THE ANSWER TO "HOW MUCH GLITTER?" IS *"yes"*

❖ ❖ ❖

Glitter. Sparkle. Fairy dust. Glitter on clothing, on the table, on your face. . . . Own it. Do it full tilt. Too much? That only means you've unleashed your inner child, and what could be better than that? Just a touch? Great, you're playful yet refined. Make your own glitter-encrusted decorations, add sparkle-encrusted twigs to your flower arrangements, hang fairy-dusted ornaments

Zac glitters a guest

from light fixtures or trees. Sparkle will brighten your surroundings, create a wonderful atmosphere for your guests, and improve your mood! In fact, we've had several employees tell us that they wear our fairy wings when they are at home—alone—when they vacuum or do the dishes. Why? Well, how can it be a chore if you're wearing fairy wings?

Glitter makes the young feel magical and the rest feel young. No one is ever too old to sparkle!

Introduction

❖ ❖ ❖

*O*nce upon a time, in a land called New York City, there were two sisters. Their father was a spinner of tales, always armed with a freshly brewed mug of English breakfast tea. Their mother was a songstress who loved to be out and about, and together, they would take the sisters to afternoon tea wherever it was served. The sisters learned at a very early age that tea was more than a beverage—it was an event to be shared and protected. Tea was a sacred experience, whether at a hotel or at home; it was a time to connect, share your thoughts and dreams, and escape for a spell.

And that is how Alice's Tea Cup came to be . . .

We, the sisters, Haley and Lauren Fox, spent our lifetimes enjoying the art of tea, from the drink itself to understanding the differences between an Assam and a Darjeeling. The act of taking afternoon tea—whether for a tea party, where friends gather to reconnect, or just as a safe haven to have a heart-to-heart with someone you love—is a true joy. Tea is a fixture in our lives, used to wake us up, keep us healthy and detoxified, add flavor to our cooking and baking, and provide a magical ambiance to share with friends.

As we became settled in our twenties, we would meet for tea and dream about a place of our own, a place where the pinky needn't be "up," where

OPPOSITE: *Lauren and Haley having tea at Chapter 1*
RIGHT, TOP AND BOTTOM: *Thanks for everything, Mom and Dad!*

Lauren, left alone with a piece of her first birthday cake

Crowding our mom as she baked, as usual! Lauren's T-shirt says "tea" on it!

Haley's sixth birthday

afternoon tea could be enjoyed before and after noon, where tea was a healthy and hearty meal that didn't leave you hungry, where people could escape from their daily grind for a nostalgic time full of whimsy and comfort, where tea was more like the upside-down tea party of the Mad Hatter's than tea at the Palm Court—a family-friendly place for the Alice in all of us. We would talk about how "someday" we would do something that would fulfill us creatively and give us the stability to follow our individual dreams.

It was almost by chance that we stumbled upon the tiny For Rent sign on Seventy-third Street off Columbus Avenue. But when we saw it, everything changed. Alice's Tea Cup opened in December 2001 to a line around the corner. It didn't hurt that Florence Fabricant had featured us on the cover of the Metro section of the *New York Times* the week before (how lucky are we?), and that many passersby had been coming in, curiouser and curiouser, to

find out what we were planning on opening there (oh, Upper West Siders are such a community-minded group!). We had a fire lit under us, with anticipation brewing like a fresh pot of Grand Keemun!

We found ourselves in this position because Haley's husband, Michael Eisenberg, a restaurant consultant, had continued to tell us to "act as if" rather than just talk about this fantasy tea salon. One day, as he had suspected, we found ourselves with a business plan, financing, and a lease that was just waiting to be signed. Michael had planned to assist us with opening and then continue consulting for others, but he hasn't left us since that day. (Thanks, Michael!) We were immediately embraced by the neighborhood as a shelter from the hustle and bustle of the city streets.

Michael Eisenberg,
our director of operations

As our popularity expanded, so did we by lengthening our hours and expanding our menus and, ultimately, by opening up two more locations (Sixty-fourth and Lexington Avenue and Eighty-first between Second and Third avenues) Alice's Tea Cup has grown from that one "little shop around the corner" that offered only afternoon tea, teapots, and loose tea to three bustling Manhattan locations, all offering breakfast, brunch, lunch, supper, and, of course, afternoon tea served before and after noon, along with little shops that sell everything from tea ware to fairy wings! All our locations host bridal and baby showers, birthday parties, and even un-birthday parties. We design and make wedding and birthday cakes and cater parties, and our bakery offers five daily scone choices, incredible cakes, cupcakes, cookies, muffins, and out-of-this-world banana bread. In 2008 we launched our gift website, where shoppers can choose anything from loose tea to unique gift boxes.

People often ask us how it is to work as a family: sister as partner, husband or brother-in-law as the director of operations—it does sound a little frightening. But for us, the family dynamic works in a way that another kind of partnership wouldn't. Our sisterly personalities are so different that we tend to view ourselves as a yin to the other's yang, each bringing her own sensibility and expertise to the table. This diversity of personality and expertise is what has made Alice's unique and accessible. But what continues to drive Alice's growth is really the staff, with their wonderful personalities and unparalleled love for our food and for creating a memorable experience for our customers. We are beyond grateful to them all, past and present, for our continued success.

Alice's Tea Cup prides itself on the unique menus we offer, full of tea infusions, beginning with our afternoon tea menu and ending with mar-tea-nis. Our philosophy is "tea turned on its ear": smoking our chicken with Lapsang Souchong, steeping our eggs in Maté Carnival, infusing our crème anglaise with Mauritius. Our scones push the limits on creative, with choices such as pumpkin with a caramel glaze, Stilton with walnuts, peanut butter and jelly, and even ginger-pear. Our brunch menu boasts such unique selections as Alice's Curious French Toast Bread Pudding and Alice's Eggs Benedict, which is served, of course, on a ham and cheese scone. This cookbook provides these easy-to-follow recipes and dozens more, and also includes tips on how to avoid waste (anything can be used to create a new variety of scone!) and suggestions on how to throw a "curiouser and curiouser" tea party with nothing other than items you already have in your cupboard.

The initial inspiration for our menu came from Lauren, who kept trying to perfect "the scone" so that we could throw our own tea parties for friends. We were tired and saddened by the impression people had of the scone: dry as a hockey puck, not a muffin but not cake but not bread . . . We took Lauren's already near-perfect scone recipe and left it in the capable hands of Sue McClinton, our

über-baker-extraordinaire, who perfected it and has been coming up with creative additions daily for almost eight years.

Our family, with mocha cake

Our scones are wildly popular in the blogosphere and beyond. Hillary Clinton was overheard telling someone on the phone how much she loved them after brunch one day, and *The Daily Show* with Jon Stewart has a standing weekly assorted scone order. *Thousands* of patrons have been asking for the recipe for years and years. So here it is . . .

Afternoon Tea, Before and After Noon: Scones

(and a Cream...)

✦ ✦ ✦

Scones. Not hockey pucks, not murder weapons, scones. Our scones are wildly popular, and it's because they're *that* good! At Alice's, we concentrate on making all foods light, fluffy, and delicious, and we make no exception with the ever-important scone. Scones may be a throwback favorite for tea aficionados, but most people are used to tolerating the scone, not truly, truly loving it. Throw out your preconceived notions about scones being dry, salty, and full of baking soda—it's time to redefine the scone. We're a tea salon, after all, and we knew our scones had to be more than just passable, more than a simple conduit for clotted cream and preserves. Our scones had to be great—and they are.

We could fill an entire book with scone recipes, but we chose to restrain ourselves and offer these nineteen classic Alice's Tea Cup scones so that we could fit in some other recipes as well!

✦ Tips ✦

In the unlikely event that you're left with uneaten scones after three days, it's time to make some wonderful biscotti! Just cut the scones into ½- to 1-inch-thick slices and bake them at 350°F for about 5 minutes on each side. For an extra treat, sprinkle a little sugar on each side before baking. Yum!

Please do not overwork the scone dough! It *should* seem slightly unmixed. This is essential to achieving the light and fluffy nature of our scones.

Pumpkin Scones

{ MAKES 10 TO 12 SCONES }

AH, THE PUMPKIN SCONE. The most discussed and praised scone on the planet. In all honesty, this scone was a happy accident of sorts. For Thanksgiving 2003, our baker, Sue McClinton, had the idea of making a pumpkin scone instead of a pumpkin cheesecake, and because of its popularity (and the fact that Haley has to have one every day), we kept it on through Christmas that year. Once the holidays were over and the mistletoe un-hung, Sue moved on to another type of scone, and all-but-rioting broke out that week when patrons discovered that there were no pumpkin scones. We heard the message loud and clear and have had pumpkin scones on the menu every day since then. In fact, pumpkin became our staple scone well before the standard and expected buttermilk scone entered our daily repertoire! Moist, slightly spicy, definitely gooey, and sweet on top (think of pumpkin pie inside a scone and you get the idea), the pumpkin scone remains a major favorite, and Haley—and now her kids—continues to have one almost each day! (In fact, Haley's son, Maddan, constantly begs to take one to school for a snack.)

These scones are best when served warm, but if you aren't serving them right away, we recommend that you don't glaze them until shortly before you serve them.

(continued)

SCONES

3 cups all-purpose flour

⅓ cup sugar

½ teaspoon baking soda

2½ teaspoons baking powder

¾ teaspoon kosher salt

¼ cup ground ginger

¼ cup ground cinnamon

1½ sticks (¾ cup) unsalted butter, cut into ½-inch pieces

1¼ cups buttermilk

1 cup canned pumpkin puree (all pumpkin, not pumpkin pie filling)

2 tablespoons pure vanilla extract

CARAMEL GLAZE

2 sticks (1 cup) unsalted butter

1 cup firmly packed light brown sugar

½ teaspoon freshly squeezed lemon juice

¼ teaspoon kosher salt

½ cup heavy cream

Sue makes Pumpkin Scones

1. Preheat the oven to 425°F.

2. In a large mixing bowl, combine the flour, sugar, baking soda, baking powder, salt, ginger, and cinnamon.

3. With clean hands, work the butter into the dry mixture until it is thoroughly incorporated and has the consistency of fine breadcrumbs.

4. Make a well in the center of the dry ingredients, and pour the buttermilk, pumpkin puree, and vanilla extract into the well. Still using your hands, combine the ingredients until all the dry mixture is wet, but do not knead!

5. Turn the mixture onto a floured surface and gather the dough together. Gently pat the dough to make a disk about 1½ inches thick. Using a 3- or 3½-inch biscuit cutter, cut out as many scones as you can and lay them on a nonstick baking sheet. Gather the remaining dough together lightly to cut out more scones—just don't knead the dough too much.

6. Bake the scones for about 12 minutes, or until lightly browned. Let the scones cool slightly on the baking sheet (about 20 minutes) before glazing them.

7. While the scones are cooling, prepare the caramel glaze: Place the butter, brown sugar, lemon juice, and salt in a saucepan over medium heat and whisk gently until the mixture is smooth. Just as the mixture comes to a light boil, add the heavy cream and reduce the heat to low. Whisk well for 2 minutes, or until the glaze is thickened and smooth; then remove the pan from the heat.

8. To glaze a scone, hold it by the bottom, dip the top in the warm caramel glaze, and place it back on the baking sheet.

Buttermilk Scones

{ MAKES 10 TO 12 SCONES }

3 cups all-purpose flour

½ teaspoon baking soda

2½ teaspoons baking powder

¾ teaspoon kosher salt

1½ sticks (¾ cup) unsalted butter, melted

¾ cup buttermilk

INITIALLY WE SERVED only sweet scones, but seriously, what were we thinking? We came to our senses, listened to our customers, and created another daily staple: the first of our savory scone offerings. This is a plain—but far from bland—buttermilk scone, something akin to a buttermilk biscuit, but in our opinion, better . . .

1. Preheat the oven to 425°F.

2. In a large mixing bowl, combine the flour, baking soda, baking powder, and salt.

3. Make a well in the center of the dry ingredients, and pour the butter and buttermilk into the well. With clean hands, combine the ingredients until all the dry mixture is wet, but do not knead!

4. Turn the mixture onto a floured surface and gather the dough together. Gently pat the dough to make a disk about 1½ inches thick. Using a 3- or 3½-inch biscuit cutter, cut out as many scones as you can and lay them on a nonstick baking sheet. Gather the remaining dough together lightly to cut out more scones—just don't knead the dough too much.

5. Bake the scones for about 12 minutes, or until lightly browned.

Black Forest Ham and Cheese Scones

{ MAKES 10 TO 12 SCONES }

3 cups all-purpose flour

¼ teaspoon baking soda

1¼ teaspoons baking powder

½ teaspoon kosher salt

½ cup diced cheddar cheese
(¼-inch dice)

½ cup diced Gruyère cheese
(¼-inch dice)

¾ cup chopped sliced Black Forest
ham (½-inch pieces)

¼ cup minced fresh chives

1¼ sticks (10 tablespoons) unsalted
butter, melted

½ cup buttermilk

THE SECOND ADDITION to our savory scone repertoire, this one has also become a daily offering at all our locations. We took two favorite all-American ingredients, fancied them up a bit, and added them to our buttermilk scone recipe. Black Forest ham, cheddar cheese, and chives make this scone irresistible! We've been told that it's very hard to eat just one of these cheesy treats.

1. Preheat the oven to 425°F.

2. In a large mixing bowl, combine the flour, baking soda, baking powder, and salt. Add the cheeses, ham, and chives to the dry mixture and combine thoroughly.

3. Make a well in the center of the dry ingredients, and pour the butter and buttermilk into the well. With clean hands, combine the ingredients until all the dry mixture is wet, but do not knead!

4. Turn the mixture onto a floured surface and gather the dough together. Gently pat the dough to make a disk about 1½ inches thick. Using a 3- or 3½-inch biscuit cutter, cut out as many scones as you can and lay them on a nonstick baking sheet. Gather the remaining dough together lightly to cut out more scones—just don't knead the dough too much.

5. Bake the scones for about 12 minutes, or until lightly browned.

Mixed Berry Scones

{ MAKES 10 TO 12 SCONES }

3 cups all-purpose flour

⅓ cup sugar

½ teaspoon baking soda

2½ teaspoons baking powder

¾ teaspoon kosher salt

1½ sticks (¾ cup) unsalted butter, cut into ½-inch pieces

½ cup blueberries

½ cup raspberries

½ cup blackberries

¼ cup hulled and quartered strawberries

1¼ cups buttermilk

1 teaspoon pure vanilla extract

¼ cup heavy cream (for brushing)

¼ cup sugar (for sprinkling)

IMAGINE THE GOODNESS of a sweet scone, then add an assortment of fresh berries to it, and the result is a sweet treat with a burst of tart yumminess. You can use the berry combination below or mix and match to find your favorite.

1. Preheat the oven to 400°F.

2. In a large mixing bowl, combine the flour, sugar, baking soda, baking powder, and salt.

3. With clean hands, work the butter into the dry mixture until it is thoroughly incorporated and has the consistency of fine breadcrumbs. Add all the berries and stir well, so that the berries are evenly distributed throughout the mixture.

4. Make a well in the center of the dry ingredients, and pour the buttermilk and vanilla extract into the well. Still using your hands, combine the ingredients until all the dry mixture is wet, but do not knead!

5. Turn the mixture onto a floured surface and gather the dough together. Gently pat the dough to make a disk about 1½ inches thick. Using a 3- or 3½-inch biscuit cutter, cut out as many scones as you can and lay them on a nonstick baking sheet. Gather the remaining dough together lightly to cut out more scones—just don't knead the dough too much.

6. Brush the top of each scone liberally with heavy cream and then sprinkle with sugar. Bake the scones for about 12 minutes, or until lightly browned.

> ◆ **Tip** ◆
>
> Don't throw away berries or other fruits that are starting to feel a little mushy—use them to make scones! Either slice them up and put them into the mixture or blend/ puree them and add them to the batter.

Walnut Stilton Scones

3 cups all-purpose flour

¼ teaspoon baking soda

1¼ teaspoons baking powder

½ teaspoon kosher salt

¾ cup crumbled Stilton cheese

¾ cup finely chopped walnuts

1¼ sticks (10 tablespoons) unsalted
   butter, melted

½ cup buttermilk

AS OUR SCONE WORLD grew, Sue created this sophisticated savory delight. Try mini versions of these scones when entertaining, served with grapes and sliced apples! Walnut pieces and the tangy boldness of Stilton cheese give this scone its complex flavor.

1. Preheat the oven to 425°F.

2. In a large mixing bowl, combine the flour, baking soda, baking powder, and salt. Add the Stilton and walnuts to the dry mixture, and combine thoroughly.

3. Make a well in the center of the dry ingredients, and pour the butter and buttermilk into the well. With clean hands, combine the ingredients until all the dry mixture is wet, but do not knead!

4. Turn the mixture onto a floured surface and gather the dough together. Gently pat the dough to make a disk about 1½ inches thick. Using a 3- or 3½-inch biscuit cutter, cut out as many scones as you can and lay them on a nonstick baking sheet. Gather the remaining dough together lightly to cut out more scones—just don't knead the dough too much.

5. Bake the scones for about 12 minutes, or until lightly browned.

Lemon Poppy Seed Scones

{ MAKES 10 TO 12 SCONES }

3 cups all-purpose flour

⅓ cup sugar

½ teaspoon baking soda

2½ teaspoons baking powder

¾ teaspoon kosher salt

1½ sticks (¾ cup) unsalted butter,
  cut into ½-inch pieces

1 tablespoon plus ¼ teaspoon
  freshly grated lemon zest

1 tablespoon poppy seeds

1¼ cups buttermilk

1 teaspoon pure vanilla extract

¼ cup heavy cream (for brushing)

¼ cup sugar (for sprinkling)

LAUREN'S UPSTAIRS NEIGHBOR pops into our Chapter I location regularly to check on whether we have these! She's a health nut (no sugar or dairy), but all bets are off where these lemony treats are concerned. In fact, she recently did a ten-day cleansing fast and asked Lauren to have the restaurant make them the first weekend off her fast! Lemon zest and crunchy poppy seeds intermingle in this dainty dandy.

1. Preheat the oven to 400°F.

2. In a large mixing bowl, combine the flour, sugar, baking soda, baking powder, and salt.

3. With clean hands, work the butter into the dry mixture until it is thoroughly incorporated and has the consistency of fine breadcrumbs. Add 1 tablespoon of the zest and the poppy seeds, and mix until the zest and poppy seeds are evenly distributed.

4. Make a well in the center of the dry ingredients, and pour the buttermilk and vanilla extract into the well. Combine the ingredients until all the dry mixture is wet, but do not knead!

5. Turn the mixture onto a floured surface and gather the dough together. Gently pat the dough to make a rectangle about 1½ inches thick. Using a dough cutter, cut the scones into wedges measuring about 3½ × 4 inches, and lay them on a nonstick baking sheet. Gather the remaining dough together lightly to cut out more scones—just don't knead the dough too much.

6. Stir the remaining ¼ teaspoon lemon zest into the heavy cream. Brush the top of each scone liberally with this mixture, and then sprinkle with sugar.

7. Bake the scones for about 12 minutes, or until lightly browned.

Peanut Butter and Jelly Scones

{ MAKES 10 TO 12 SCONES }

3 cups all-purpose flour

⅓ cup sugar

½ teaspoon baking soda

2½ teaspoons baking powder

¾ teaspoon kosher salt

1½ sticks (¾ cup) unsalted butter,
  cut into ½-inch pieces

1¼ cups buttermilk

½ cup creamy peanut butter

½ cup raspberry, strawberry,
  or grape preserves

1 teaspoon pure vanilla extract

¼ cup heavy cream (for brushing)

¼ cup sugar (for sprinkling)

ONE OF LAUREN'S all-time favorite scones, this one is a bit mind-blowing in its execution. Just imagine: a peanut butter and jelly sandwich in a scone! Salty peanut butter and sweet raspberry jam are interlaced throughout this tasty treat. A glass of milk, and you will be transported . . .

1. Preheat the oven to 425°F.

2. In a large mixing bowl, combine the flour, sugar, baking soda, baking powder, and salt.

3. With clean hands, work the butter into the dry mixture until it is thoroughly incorporated and has the consistency of fine breadcrumbs.

4. Make a well in the center of the dry ingredients, and add the buttermilk, peanut butter, preserves, and vanilla extract to the well. Do not worry about incorporating the ingredients too well; the goal is to get bites of peanut butter and jelly throughout. Combine the ingredients until all the dry mixture is wet, but do not knead!

5. Turn the mixture onto a floured surface and gather the dough together. Gently pat the dough to make a disk about 1½ inches thick. Using a 3- or 3½-inch biscuit cutter, cut out as many scones as you can and lay them on a nonstick baking sheet. Gather the remaining dough together lightly to cut out more scones—just don't knead the dough too much.

6. Brush the top of each scone liberally with heavy cream and then sprinkle with sugar.

7. Bake the scones for about 12 minutes, or until lightly browned.

Berry Bunch Tisane—Infused Scones

{ MAKES 10 TO 12 SCONES }

1 heaping tablespoon Berry Bunch
  Tisane (see Resources)

3 cups all-purpose flour

⅓ cup sugar

½ teaspoon baking soda

2½ teaspoons baking powder

¾ teaspoon kosher salt

1½ sticks (¾ cup) unsalted butter,
  cut into ½-inch pieces

¼ cup blueberries

¼ cup raspberries

¼ cup blackberries

1¼ cups buttermilk

½ teaspoon pure vanilla extract

¼ cup heavy cream (for brushing)

¼ cup sugar (for sprinkling)

WE ARE OBSESSED with tea infusions and encourage our bakers to experiment with them all the time. One such experiment with Berry Bunch (technically a tisane, not a tea) yielded these funky, fabulous scones. Lauren thinks they taste like several fruity breakfast cereals she remembers from childhood. Haley thinks they taste like Pop-Tarts. What do you think?

1. Preheat the oven to 425°F.

2. Steep the Berry Bunch Tisane in ¼ cup boiling-hot water for 7 minutes. Strain, and reserve the tea.

3. In a large mixing bowl, combine the flour, sugar, baking soda, baking powder, and salt.

4. With clean hands, work the butter into the dry mixture until it is thoroughly incorporated and has the consistency of fine breadcrumbs. Add all the berries and combine well, so that they are evenly distributed throughout the dry mixture.

5. Make a well in the center of the dry ingredients, and pour the buttermilk, vanilla extract, and 1 tablespoon of the tea into the well. Combine the ingredients until all the dry mixture is wet, but do not knead!

6. Turn the mixture onto a floured surface and gather the dough together. Gently pat the dough to make a rectangle about 1½ inches thick. Using a dough cutter, cut into wedges measuring about 3½ × 4 inches, and lay them on a nonstick baking sheet. Gather the remaining dough together lightly to cut out more scones—just don't knead the dough too much.

7. Brush the top of each scone liberally with heavy cream and then sprinkle with sugar.

8. Bake the scones for about 12 minutes, or until lightly browned.

Turtle Scones

{ MAKES 10 TO 12 SCONES }

3 cups all-purpose flour

⅓ cup sugar

½ teaspoon baking soda

2½ teaspoons baking powder

¾ teaspoon kosher salt

1½ sticks (¾ cup) unsalted butter, cut into ½-inch pieces

¾ cup pecans, finely chopped

¾ cup dark chocolate pistoles or semisweet chocolate chunks (see Note)

1¼ cups buttermilk

1 teaspoon pure vanilla extract

Caramel Glaze (page 11)

A RECENT ADDITION to the Alice's menu, this scone has fast become one of our most popular. It's no surprise, since it's more dessert than scone—full of chocolate chips and nuts and drenched in caramel (think the blondie of scones). Yum . . . but prepare to get sticky fingers!

These scones are best when served warm, but if you aren't serving them right away, we recommend that you don't glaze them until shortly before you serve them.

1. Preheat the oven to 425°F.

2. In a large mixing bowl, combine the flour, sugar, baking soda, baking powder, and salt.

3. With clean hands, work the butter into the dry mixture until it is thoroughly incorporated and has the consistency of fine breadcrumbs. Add the pecans and chocolate and combine well, so that they are evenly distributed throughout the dry mixture.

4. Make a well in the center of the dry ingredients, and pour the buttermilk and vanilla extract into the well. Combine the ingredients until all the dry mixture is wet, but do not knead!

5. Turn the mixture onto a floured surface and gather the dough together. Gently pat the dough to make a rectangle about 1½ inches thick. Using a dough cutter, cut the scones into wedges measuring about 3½ × 4 inches, and lay them on a nonstick baking sheet. Gather the remaining dough together lightly to cut out more scones—just don't knead the dough too much.

6. Bake the scones for about 12 minutes, or until lightly browned. Let the scones cool slightly (about 20 minutes) on the baking sheet before glazing.

7. To glaze a scone, hold it by the bottom, dip the top in the caramel glaze, and place it back on the baking sheet.

NOTE: We recommend Cacao Barry Dark "Favorites Mi-Amère" Pistoles if you can get them. If not, Baker's Semi-Sweet Chocolate will also work.

"As a British citizen living in America, I am always on the lookout to find the perfect scone, the perfect cup of tea, and the perfect place to buy fairy wings. I eventually found Alice's Tea Cup, which has the best examples of all three that you will ever find without having to chase a white rabbit down a hole and into the New York subway system. I take my family to Alice's whenever they come to visit me, to prove to them that Americans can make a flawless cup of tea and that the War of Independence was therefore not a total waste."

—John Oliver

Lavender Earl Grey Scones

{ MAKES 10 TO 12 SCONES }

2 heaping teaspoons Lavender Earl Grey tea leaves (see Resources)

3 cups all-purpose flour

⅓ cup sugar

½ teaspoon baking soda

2½ teaspoons baking powder

¾ teaspoon kosher salt

1½ sticks (¾ cup) unsalted butter, cut into ½-inch pieces

1¼ cups buttermilk

½ teaspoon pure vanilla extract

¼ cup heavy cream (for brushing)

¼ cup sugar (for sprinkling)

THIS IS ONE of Haley's favorites, not only because she's an Earl Grey drinker (in fact, as a bitty child she would ask the waitresses in diners if the tea was Earl Grey or orange pekoe because she "simply wouldn't drink anything but Earl Grey"—precocious much?) but also because the hint of lavender infusion leaves you feeling as if you ate a scone and then walked through a field *en Provence*!

1. Preheat the oven to 425°F.

2. Steep 1 heaping teaspoon of the Lavender Earl Grey tea leaves in ¼ cup boiling-hot water for 3 minutes. Strain, and reserve the tea.

3. In a coffee or spice grinder, grind the remaining teaspoon of Lavender Earl Grey tea leaves to a very fine powder. Place the powder in a large mixing bowl, and add the flour, sugar, baking soda, baking powder, and salt. Stir until combined.

4. With clean hands, work the butter into the dry mixture until it is thoroughly incorporated and has the consistency of fine breadcrumbs.

5. Make a well in the center of the dry ingredients, and pour the buttermilk, vanilla extract, and 1 tablespoon of the brewed Lavender Earl Grey tea into the well. Combine the ingredients until all the dry mix is wet, but do not knead!

6. Turn the mixture onto a floured surface and gather the dough together. Gently pat the dough to make a rectangle about 1½ inches thick. Using a dough cutter, cut the scones into wedges measuring about 3½ × 4 inches, and lay them on a nonstick baking sheet. Gather the remaining dough together lightly to cut out more scones—just don't knead the dough too much.

7. Brush the top of each scone liberally with heavy cream and then sprinkle with sugar.

8. Bake the scones for about 12 minutes, or until lightly browned.

✦ ✦ ✦

Oatmeal Scones

{ MAKES 10 TO 12 SCONES }

3 cups all-purpose flour

⅓ cup sugar

½ teaspoon baking soda

2½ teaspoons baking powder

¾ teaspoon kosher salt

1 teaspoon ground cinnamon

1½ sticks (¾ cup) unsalted butter, cut into ½-inch pieces

1 cup dry quick-cooking Irish oatmeal (such as McCann's)

1½ cups buttermilk

2 teaspoons pure vanilla extract

¼ cup heavy cream (for brushing)

¼ cup sugar (for sprinkling)

WHOLE OATS MAKE these scones special. They can be a bit crunchy in places and chewy in others, which makes for a diverse experience within one scone. They're slightly sweet, but not a dessert scone at all.

1. Preheat the oven to 425°F.

2. In a large mixing bowl, combine the flour, sugar, baking soda, baking powder, salt, and cinnamon.

3. With clean hands, work the butter into the dry mixture until it is thoroughly incorporated and has the consistency of fine breadcrumbs. Add the oatmeal and stir well.

4. Make a well in the center of the dry ingredients, and pour the buttermilk and vanilla extract into the well. Combine the ingredients until all the dry mixture is wet, but do not knead!

5. Turn the mixture onto a floured surface and gather the dough together. Gently pat the dough to make a disk about 1½ inches thick. Using a 3- or 3¼-inch biscuit cutter, cut out as many scones as you can and lay them on a nonstick baking sheet. Gather the remaining dough together lightly to cut out more scones—just don't knead the dough too much.

6. Brush the top of each scone liberally with heavy cream and then sprinkle with sugar.

7. Bake the scones for about 12 minutes, or until lightly browned.

Vanilla Bean Scones

{ MAKES 10 TO 12 SCONES }

3 cups all-purpose flour

⅓ cup sugar

½ teaspoon baking soda

2½ teaspoons baking powder

¾ teaspoon kosher salt

1½ sticks (¾ cup) unsalted butter, cut into ½-inch pieces

2 or 3 vanilla beans, seeds scraped out and pods reserved

1¼ cups buttermilk

1 teaspoon pure vanilla extract

¼ cup heavy cream (for brushing)

¼ cup sugar (for sprinkling)

WHAT AN AMAZING scone! These can get kind of pricey because it's best to use real vanilla beans here, and scraping the seeds out of a vanilla pod doesn't amount to a hill o' beans (wink)! But real vanilla beans, especially fresh ones, are so incredibly potent that it doesn't take a whole lot to create that wonderful flavor. If you enjoy vanilla (we mean *real* vanilla, not that imitation stuff), this is your scone!

1. Preheat the oven to 425°F.

2. In a large mixing bowl, combine the flour, sugar, baking soda, baking powder, and salt.

3. With clean hands, work the butter into the dry mixture until it is thoroughly incorporated and has the consistency of fine breadcrumbs. Add the vanilla seeds (not the pods!) and combine well, so that they're evenly distributed throughout the dry mixture.

4. Make a well in the center of the dry ingredients, and pour the buttermilk and vanilla extract into the well. Combine the ingredients until all the dry mixture is wet, but do not knead!

5. Turn the mixture onto a floured surface and gather the dough together. Gently pat the dough to make a rectangle about 1½ inches thick. Using a dough cutter, cut the scones into wedges measuring about 3½ × 4 inches, and lay them on a nonstick baking sheet. Gather the remaining dough together lightly to cut out more scones—just don't knead the dough too much.

6. Brush the top of each scone liberally with heavy cream and then sprinkle with sugar.

7. Bake the scones for about 12 minutes, or until lightly browned.

Peppermint Stick Scones

{ MAKES 10 TO 12 SCONES }

3 cups all-purpose flour

⅓ cup sugar

½ teaspoon baking soda

2½ teaspoons baking powder

¾ teaspoon kosher salt

1½ sticks (¾ cup) unsalted butter,
  cut into ½-inch pieces

1 cup crushed Brach's peppermint
  Star Brites (or similar candy)

1¼ cups buttermilk

1 teaspoon pure vanilla extract

¼ cup heavy cream (for brushing)

A HOLIDAY FAVORITE, these scones really work best when you use small Brach's peppermint Star Brites, not peppermint sticks or candy canes. First, they're easier to crush, and second, they melt well—don't ask why. The fun in this scone comes from enjoying a sweet buttermilk scone and then getting hit with a surprise bit of holiday peppermint flavor!

1. Preheat the oven to 425°F.

2. In a large mixing bowl, combine the flour, sugar, baking soda, baking powder, and salt.

3. With clean hands, work the butter into the dry mixture until it is thoroughly incorporated and has the consistency of fine breadcrumbs. Add ¾ cup of the crushed peppermint candy and combine well, so that it is evenly distributed throughout the dry mixture.

4. Make a well in the center of the dry ingredients, and pour the buttermilk and vanilla extract into the well. Combine the ingredients until all the dry mixture is wet, but do not knead!

5. Turn the mixture onto a floured surface and gather the dough together. Gently pat the dough to make a rectangle about 1½ inches thick. Using a dough cutter, cut the scones into wedges measuring about 3½ × 4 inches, and lay them on a nonstick baking sheet. Gather the remaining dough together lightly to cut out more scones—just don't knead the dough too much.

6. Brush the top of each scone liberally with heavy cream, and sprinkle them with the remaining ¼ cup crushed peppermint candy.

7. Bake the scones for about 12 minutes, or until lightly browned.

Chocolate Strawberry Scones

{ MAKES 10 TO 12 SCONES }

3 cups all-purpose flour

⅓ cup sugar

½ teaspoon baking soda

2½ teaspoons baking powder

¾ teaspoon kosher salt

1½ sticks (¾ cup) unsalted butter,
cut into ½-inch pieces

1¼ cups hulled and quartered
strawberries

¾ cup dark chocolate pistoles
or semisweet chocolate chunks
(see Note)

1¼ cups buttermilk

1 teaspoon pure vanilla extract

¼ cup heavy cream (for brushing)

¼ cup sugar (for sprinkling)

A TRUE FAVORITE for our regulars—moist, simple, slightly sweet, and very fresh tasting. The strawberries provide a nice tangy sweetness, but most people just look for the bites with the warm chips in them!

1. Preheat the oven to 425°F.

2. In a large mixing bowl, combine the flour, sugar, baking soda, baking powder, and salt.

3. With clean hands, work the butter into the dry mixture until it is thoroughly incorporated and has the consistency of fine breadcrumbs. Add the strawberries and chocolate and combine well, so that they are evenly distributed throughout the dry mixture.

4. Make a well in the center of the dry ingredients, and pour the buttermilk and vanilla into the well. Combine the ingredients until all the dry mixture is wet, but do not knead!

5. Turn the mixture onto a floured surface and gather the dough together. Gently pat the dough to make a rectangle about 1½ inches thick. Using a dough cutter, cut the scones into wedges measuring about 3½ 4 inches, and lay them on a nonstick baking sheet. Gather the remaining dough together lightly to cut out more scones—just don't knead the dough too much.

6. Brush the top of each scone liberally with heavy cream and then sprinkle with sugar.

7. Bake the scones for about 12 minutes, or until lightly browned.

NOTE: We recommend Cacao Barry Dark "Favorites Mi-Amère" Pistoles if you can get them. If not, Baker's Semi-Sweet Chocolate will also work.

Bacon Cheddar Scones

{ MAKES 10 TO 12 SCONES }

3 cups all-purpose flour

¼ teaspoon baking soda

1¼ teaspoons baking powder

½ teaspoon kosher salt

1 cup diced cheddar cheese
(¼-inch dice)

¾ cup crumbled well-done (but not
burned) bacon (see Note)

1¼ sticks (10 tablespoons)
unsalted butter, melted

½ cup buttermilk

OUR BAKER OLIVER added this one kind of late in the game, after Sue's Black Forest Ham and Cheese Scones had become a daily staple. Shaking things up a bit, this scone is a breakfast in and of itself—but it is always good with eggs, of course.

1. Preheat the oven to 425°F.

2. In a large mixing bowl, combine the flour, baking soda, baking powder, and salt. Add the cheese and bacon to the dry mixture, and combine thoroughly.

3. Make a well in the center of the dry ingredients, and pour the butter and buttermilk into the well. With clean hands, combine the ingredients until all the dry mixture is wet, but do not knead!

4. Turn the mixture onto a floured surface and gather the dough together. Gently pat the dough to make a disk about 1½ inches thick. Using a 3- or 3½-inch biscuit cutter, cut out as many scones as you can and lay them on a nonstick baking sheet. Gather the remaining dough together lightly to cut out more scones—just don't knead the dough too much.

5. Bake for about 12 minutes, or until lightly browned.

NOTE: For all the bacon fanatics out there, you can add extra bacon flavor by substituting 2 tablespoons of the bacon fat left over from frying the bacon for 2 tablespoons of the butter.

Cinnascones

{ MAKES 10 TO 12 SCONES }

SCONES

3½ cups all-purpose flour

½ cup sugar

¾ teaspoon baking soda

1¾ teaspoons baking powder

¾ teaspoon kosher salt

1½ teaspoons ground cinnamon

¾ teaspoon ground nutmeg

1¼ sticks (10 tablespoons) unsalted
   butter, cut into ½-inch pieces

½ cup buttermilk

¾ teaspoon almond extract

¼ cup heavy cream (for brushing)

CINNAMON PASTE

½ stick (¼ cup) unsalted butter

½ cup firmly packed light brown
   sugar

1½ teaspoons ground cinnamon

FROSTING DRIZZLE

1 cup confectioners' sugar

2½ tablespoons whole milk

½ teaspoon almond extract

ANOTHER ONE OF Oliver's creations! Clearly fresh from a trip to Cinnabon, Oliver created another one of those scones that people are calling ahead to ask about. With sweetened cinnamon rolled into the coils of this scone, and a simple royal icing glaze on top, these were immediately consumed by everyone on our photo shoot team directly after they came off the cooling rack! They're just irresistible. Note that these are best served warm.

1. Preheat the oven to 400°F.

2. In a large mixing bowl, combine the flour, sugar, baking soda, baking powder, salt, cinnamon, and nutmeg.

3. With clean hands, work the butter into the dry mixture until it is thoroughly incorporated and has the consistency of fine breadcrumbs.

4. Make a well in the center of the dry mixture, and pour the buttermilk and almond extract into the well. Still using your hands, mix the ingredients until all the wet ingredients are absorbed by the dry. Then knead the mixture about 7 times—no more.

5. Turn the dough out onto a floured surface, and using a floured rolling pin, roll it out to form a ½-inch-thick rectangle.

6. Make the cinnamon paste by combining the butter, brown sugar, and cinnamon in a small saucepan over low heat and stirring until the sugar is completely dissolved.

7. Smear the cinnamon paste over the entire surface of the rolled-out dough. Starting at the one long side, roll the dough tightly to create a long cylinder. Using an

extremely sharp knife, slice the roll into 1-inch-thick disks. Lay the disks on their sides, spacing them about 2 inches apart, on a nonstick baking sheet. Carefully press them with the palm of your hand to flatten them to ½ inch thick.

8. Using a pastry brush, brush the tops of the disks liberally with the heavy cream.

9. Reduce the oven temperature to 350°F and bake the scones for 15 to 20 minutes, or until firm and golden on top. Remove from the oven and let cool on the baking sheet for about 20 minutes.

10. To make the frosting drizzle, combine the confectioners' sugar, milk, and almond extract in a medium bowl and whisk until smooth.

11. Using a spoon or a pastry bag, drizzle the tops of the Cinnascones in whatever design moves you!

Oliver icing Cinnascones at Chapter II

Banana Butterscotch Scones

{ MAKES 10 TO 12 SCONES }

3 cups all-purpose flour

⅓ cup sugar

½ teaspoon baking soda

2½ teaspoons baking powder

¾ teaspoon kosher salt

1½ sticks (¾ cup) unsalted butter,
    cut into ½-inch pieces

2 bananas, sliced

½ cup Hershey's butterscotch chips

1¼ cups buttermilk

1 teaspoon pure vanilla extract

¼ cup heavy cream (for brushing)

¼ cup sugar (for sprinkling)

WHAT BEGAN AS two separate scones—one with banana slices and one with butterscotch chips—got merged into one singularly spectacular scone. These flavors are pure bliss together.

1. Preheat the oven to 425°F.

2. In a large mixing bowl, combine the flour, sugar, baking soda, baking powder, and salt.

3. With clean hands, work the butter into the dry mixture until it is thoroughly incorporated and has the consistency of fine breadcrumbs. Add the banana slices and butterscotch chips and combine well, so that they are evenly distributed throughout the dry mixture.

4. Make a well in the center of the dry ingredients, and pour the buttermilk and vanilla extract into the well. Combine the ingredients until all the dry mixture is wet, but do not knead!

5. Turn the mixture onto a floured surface and gather the dough together. Gently pat the dough to make a disk about 1½ inches thick. Using a 3- or 3½-inch biscuit cutter, cut out as many scones as you can and lay them on a nonstick baking sheet. Gather the remaining dough together lightly to cut out more scones—just don't knead the dough too much.

6. Brush the top of each scone liberally with heavy cream and then sprinkle with sugar.

7. Bake the scones for about 12 minutes, or until lightly browned.

Mocha Chocolate Chip Scones

{ MAKES 10 TO 12 SCONES }

2 heaping teaspoons Medaglia
    D'Oro instant espresso powder

3 cups all-purpose flour

⅓ cup sugar

½ teaspoon baking soda

2½ teaspoons baking powder

¾ teaspoon kosher salt

1½ sticks (¾ cup) unsalted butter,
    cut into ½-inch pieces

¾ cup Hershey's semisweet
    chocolate chips

1¼ cups buttermilk

½ teaspoon pure vanilla extract

¼ cup heavy cream (for brushing)

¼ cup sugar (for sprinkling)

SERIOUSLY? SERIOUSLY. We adore Medaglia D'Oro instant espresso for its fine dust and amazingly strong flavor. You can substitute your favorite instant espresso, but Medaglia D'Oro really does make a difference.

1. Preheat the oven to 425°F.

2. Dissolve the espresso powder in 1 tablespoon hot water. Set it aside.

3. In a large mixing bowl, combine the flour, sugar, baking soda, baking powder, and salt.

4. With clean hands, work the butter into the dry mixture until it is thoroughly incorporated and has the consistency of fine breadcrumbs. Add the chocolate chips and combine well, so that they are evenly distributed throughout the dry mixture.

5. Make a well in the center of the dry ingredients, and pour the buttermilk, espresso, and vanilla extract into the well. Combine the ingredients until all the dry mixture is wet, but do not knead!

6. Turn the mixture onto a floured surface and gather the dough together. Gently pat the dough to make a rectangle about 1½ inches thick. Using a dough cutter, cut the scones into wedges measuring about 3½ × 4 inches, and lay them on a nonstick baking sheet. Gather the remaining dough together lightly to cut out more scones—just don't knead the dough too much.

7. Brush the top of each scone liberally with heavy cream and then sprinkle with sugar.

8. Bake the scones for about 12 minutes, or until lightly browned.

Rice Krispies Treats Scones

{ MAKES 10 TO 12 SCONES }

3 cups all-purpose flour

⅓ cup sugar

½ teaspoon baking soda

2½ teaspoons baking powder

¾ teaspoon kosher salt

*1½ sticks (¾ cup) unsalted butter,
    cut into ½-inch pieces*

1½ cups mini marshmallows

1 cup Rice Krispies

1¼ cups buttermilk

½ teaspoon pure vanilla extract

¼ cup heavy cream (for brushing)

¼ cup sugar (for sprinkling)

YEAH, SOUNDS WEIRD, right? Well, Lauren thought so too when our amazing former cook, Jason, proposed it one day. Her response? "Please, no." He brought it up a couple days later, and she thought for a second and said, "Sounds gross, Jason—sorry." Well, one day soon after that, actor Victor Garber was eating at Alice's when Lauren came in, said hello, and noticed that he was eating a scone she didn't recognize. Victor volunteered, "This scone is incredible, by the way . . ." Guess what it was? Lauren thanked Victor and laughed out loud, with Jason watching from the sidelines and wearing a guilty grin. (Lauren took one home with her that day and agreed that it was incredible. So, thanks, Jason! We miss you—and you, too, Victor!)

1. Preheat the oven to 425°F.

2. In a large mixing bowl, combine the flour, sugar, baking soda, baking powder, and salt.

3. With clean hands, work the butter into the dry mixture until it is thoroughly incorporated and has the consistency of fine breadcrumbs. Add the marshmallows and Rice Krispies, and combine until they are evenly distributed.

4. Make a well in the center of the dry ingredients, and pour the buttermilk and vanilla extract into the well. Combine the ingredients until all the dry mixture is just wet. Do not knead, and do not let the dough sit for long!

5. Turn the mixture onto a floured surface and gather the dough together. Gently pat the dough to make a rectangle about 1½ inches thick. Using a dough cutter, cut the scones into wedges measuring about 3½ × 4 inches, and lay them on a nonstick baking sheet. Gather the remaining dough together lightly to cut out more scones—just don't knead the dough too much.

6. Brush the top of each scone liberally with heavy cream and then sprinkle with sugar.

7. Bake the scones for about 12 minutes, or until lightly browned.

✦ ✦ ✦

Alice's "Un-clotted" Cream

1 quart heavy cream

3½ cups confectioners' sugar

⅔ cup freshly squeezed lemon juice

TANGY AND REMINISCENT of whipped cream (not the traditional English butter-style cream), this is perfect with all our sweet scones!

Pour the heavy cream into a mixer fitted with a whipping attachment. Start the mixer on medium speed and add the sugar slowly, until the entire amount is incorporated into the cream. Then add the lemon juice to the mixture in a slow stream. Turn the mixer up to high speed (taking care that the whip won't spray the ingredients out of the bowl), and whip until it forms stiff peaks—but no longer, or it will turn into butter! The cream will keep, covered, in the refrigerator for a week.

Breakfast and Brunch

✦ ✦ ✦

Our favorite mealtimes are breakfast and brunch. They are just as eventful as afternoon tea and just as tasty, but a great breakfast or brunch experience can also make your day! When we were little girls, our mother was big on the Saturday-/Sunday-morning breakfast/brunch ritual at home (by the time we were teenagers, she had put the pans aside and we had become regulars at local brunch spots on the Upper West Side). We remember happily making waffles and pancakes, various egg dishes, and, yes, the occasional scone with Mom. In all honesty, she really only had us cracking eggs and pouring in milk, but it was a thrill to crowd around her in the kitchen. Even when our friends came over and she had several excited children hanging from her waist, it never seemed to bother her. Those breakfasts always left us feeling as if we'd begun our day by creating something incredible!

When it came time to think about breakfast and brunch at Alice's, we couldn't help but remember our breakfast rituals at home, and the staples we all love and crave. And then, as usual, we pondered them "through the looking glass . . ."

So, invite your kids into the kitchen, pull up that stool (but keep it a safe distance from the stove—thanks, Mom!), and create some memories.

Stevie chalks it up!

Alice's Eggs Benedict and Potato-Chicken Hash

{ MAKES 1 SERVING }

1 savory scone (we recommend the Black Forest Ham and Cheese, page 13)

1 teaspoon distilled white vinegar

2 eggs

¼ cup Hollandaise Sauce (recipe follows)

½ cup Potato-Chicken Hash (page 38)

WHEN WE CREATED our brunch menu, we definitely wanted to include that brunch staple, the Benedict, but in sticking with our zany ways, we put those poached babies atop a ham and cheese scone instead of the standard, boring old English muffin, and we bypassed the Canadian bacon altogether! The hash is so flavorful and filling, you could actually make it the meal! Our wonderfully smoky Lapsang Souchong Chicken Breast is sautéed to perfection with potatoes and rosemary. Many of our friends have a love/hate relationship with this truly decadent, not-at-all-lo-cal brunch sensation, but our motto is: Everything in moderation. This one can't be ignored, so put that poached egg on that scone, drizzle it with hollandaise sauce, and dig in . . .

1. Preheat the oven to 300°F.

2. Using a sharp knife, cut the scone in half horizontally. Put the scone halves in the oven and reduce the temperature to 250°F. Heat the scone halves for 2 to 4 minutes, making sure they don't brown or burn.

3. While the scone halves are warming, fill a small saucepan one-fourth full with water and add the vinegar (it will help to keep the egg yolks together). Bring the water to a simmer over medium heat. One at a time, break the eggs into a small bowl and then carefully slip them into the water. Cook for 1 to 2 minutes, or until the whites have firmed but the yolks are still soft. Remove the eggs with a slotted spoon, letting the water drain away.

4. Set the warm scone halves on a dinner plate and place an egg on each one. Drizzle the Hollandaise Sauce over the eggs, and serve with the Potato-Chicken Hash on the side.

HOLLANDAISE SAUCE

{ MAKES APPROXIMATELY
1½ CUPS }

2½ sticks (1¼ cups) unsalted butter

3 egg yolks

¾ teaspoon freshly squeezed lemon
 juice

¾ teaspoon heavy cream, plus
 additional as needed

Leaves from 1 small sprig fresh
 rosemary, finely minced

Kosher salt and freshly ground
 black pepper

1. First, clarify the butter: Melt the butter in a microwave oven, or in a Pyrex measuring cup set in a hot water bath, until the milk fat settles on the bottom. The clarified butter is the clear yellow butter on the top. Pour this into a measuring cup; you should have about 1 cup clarified butter. Set it aside and discard the milk fat.

2. For this next step, you need to create a bain-marie (water bath). There are two ways to do it:

   1. Take a large pot and put a smaller metal or glass mixing bowl inside it. Fill the pot with water, so the level reaches about half the height of the mixing bowl—no more. Be careful not to get water in the mixing bowl. Put the pot on the stove over low to medium heat.

   2. Or try Lauren's favorite method: use a slow cooker! You'll need a little more time, but this method makes a gentler, more controlled heat. Just place a bowl in the cooker and pour water into the cooker as described above. Turn the heat to medium to heat the water.

3. When the water in the water bath is very hot, place the egg yolks and lemon juice in the mixing bowl and whisk until the mixture is almost emulsified, about 1 minute. Pour the clarified butter into the egg mixture in a thin drizzle, whisking constantly and taking care not to spill the mixture into the water, or vice versa. When the mixture has cooked and thickened slightly, add the cream, rosemary, and salt and pepper to taste, still whisking constantly until fully combined.

4. To keep the sauce warm until serving, let the bowl sit in the hot water bath (on the lowest heat setting). If the sauce gets too hot and starts to separate, whisk in a little more heavy cream.

POTATO-CHICKEN HASH

{ MAKES 4 TO 5 CUPS }

3 large unpeeled Idaho (baking) potatoes, well washed, cut into ¾-inch cubes and placed in a bowl of cold water

1 stick (½ cup) butter, melted

2 teaspoons minced fresh rosemary

Kosher salt and freshly ground black pepper

2 Lapsang Souchong Smoked Chicken breasts (page 78), cut into ¾-47inch cubes

1. Preheat the oven to 400°F.

2. Bring a large pot of salted water to a boil. Add the potatoes and cook over medium heat until they are about halfway cooked (fork-tender but not falling apart).

3. Drain the potatoes and spread them out on a rimmed baking sheet. Pour the melted butter over the potatoes, sprinkle them with the rosemary, and season with salt and pepper to taste. Roast the potatoes until they are browned and tender, 12 to 15 minutes.

4. In a saucepan over medium heat, add a small pat of butter, the potatoes, and the chicken and saute for about 2 minutes, or until hash is very slightly browned. Serve immediately.

Ingrid takes Eggs Benedict very seriously!

Alice's Eggs Florentine

{ MAKES 1 SERVING }

2 handfuls raw spinach

1 savory scone (we recommend Buttermilk, page 12)

2 eggs

1 teaspoon distilled white vinegar

¼ cup Hollandaise Sauce (page 37)

½ cup Asparagus and Pears (page 40)

THIS BRUNCH FAVORITE gets a twist, with all of its components—a poached egg, sautéed spinach, and hollandaise sauce—atop a buttermilk scone. It's just as decadent and tasty as the Benedict, *sans* meat and cheese, and with the added bonus of iron from the spinach! After all, you've got to have your daily serving of greens, and we ask, is there a better (translation: yummier) way to get 'em?

1. Preheat the oven to 300°F.

2. Wash the spinach leaves well under cold water and remove the stems. Place the spinach and 1 or 2 tablespoons water in a medium saucepan, cover, and cook over low heat for about 5 minutes, or until the leaves are limp and dark green. Drain the spinach well and set it aside.

3. Using a sharp knife, cut the scone in half horizontally. Put the scone halves in the oven and reduce the temperature to 250°F. Heat the scone halves for 2 to 4 minutes, making sure they don't brown or burn.

4. While the scone halves are warming, fill a small saucepan one-fourth full with water, and add the vinegar (it will help to keep the egg yolks together). Bring the water to a simmer over medium heat. One at a time, break the eggs into a small bowl and then carefully slip them into the water. Cook for 1 to 2 minutes, or until the whites have firmed but the yolks are still soft. Remove the eggs with a slotted spoon, letting the water drain away.

5. Set the warm scone halves on a dinner plate, and distribute the steamed spinach evenly between them. Place a poached egg on each scone half. Drizzle the Hollandaise Sauce over the eggs, and serve with a side of Asparagus and Pears.

ASPARAGUS AND PEARS

{ MAKES 4 SERVINGS }

3 or 4 Anjou pears

3 tablespoons butter, melted

1 tablespoon freshly squeezed lemon juice

Kosher salt and freshly ground black pepper

12 asparagus spears

1 tablespoon canola oil

1. Preheat the oven to 350°F.

2. Core the pears (but do not peel them) and cut them into ¼-inch dice. As you cut them, place them in a bowl of cold water to prevent them from oxidizing. Then drain the pears and toss them in a bowl with the butter, lemon juice, and salt and pepper to taste. Spread the pears on a baking sheet and roast in the oven until the edges start to brown, 10 to 12 minutes.

3. While the pears are roasting, cut the tough bottom ends off the asparagus spears. Toss the asparagus in the oil, and season with salt and pepper to taste.

4. When the pears are done and you are ready to serve, sauté the pears and asparagus together in a medium saucepan over medium heat until the asparagus is slightly tender but not soft, about 3 minutes.

5. Serve hot.

NOTES:

You can store the cooked pears and the marinated asparagus separately for several days and then sauté them just before you're ready to serve.

This dish isn't solely limited to a breakfast side. It is the perfect complement to grilled chicken, fish, or steak. For a healthy vegetarian meal, try it over a bed of quinoa or brown rice— so delicious!

Alice's Blueberry Cornmeal Pancakes

{ MAKES 16 TO 18 PANCAKES,
TO SERVE 4 }

2 cups all-purpose flour

1½ cups yellow cornmeal

½ cup sugar

1 teaspoon baking soda

2½ tablespoons baking powder

1 teaspoon salt

3 cups buttermilk

⅓ cup plus 1 tablespoon unsalted butter, melted

4 eggs, lightly beaten

1½ cups blueberries

THESE PANCAKES TRULY rock our world. The cornmeal makes them light and fluffy, with a slight crisp to the top and bottom. Add to that the constant explosion of tart fresh blueberries, and these are sure to satisfy any pancake aficionado! Just add real maple syrup and prepare to become obsessed . . .

1. In a large bowl, mix the flour, cornmeal, sugar, baking soda, baking powder, and salt. Pour the buttermilk, butter, and eggs into the dry mixture and mix well with a spatula until all lumps are smoothed out (do not use a whisk or a mixer). Let the mixture sit for 15 minutes. Mix again with a spatula, and let it sit for another 15 minutes.

2. Place a nonstick frying pan or griddle over medium heat. Using a ¼-cup measure or a 2-ounce scoop, pour the batter into the pan to make pancakes (work in batches and do not crowd the pancakes). Add 6 or 7 blueberries to the top of each pancake and gently press them in. When bubbles start to burst on the top of a pancake, flip it over with a spatula and cook for about 1 minute.

3. To keep the pancakes warm while you make the rest of them, put them on an oven-safe plate in a warm oven.

Alice's Fruit Omelet

{ MAKES 1 SERVING }

2 eggs

1 pinch kosher salt

1 tablespoon unsalted butter

1 cup mixed berries (strawberries, blueberries, raspberries, and/or blackberries)

WHO SAYS FRUIT and eggs don't mix? Not us! This breakfast offering came out of our love of omelets and our desire for something, *anything*, that would give us a break from the standard omelet ingredients. We're huge fans of sweet and savory all in one bite, and this number certainly does the trick, with a tart kick thrown in as a bonus! A light and healthy omelet filled with fresh mixed berries—it's as simple (yet complex) as that.

1. Whisk the eggs and salt together in a small mixing bowl.

2. Melt the butter in a nonstick frying pan over medium heat until it sizzles. Pour the egg mixture into the pan and swirl it around to cover the bottom of the pan. As the omelet cooks, lift the cooked edges frequently with a spatula to let the excess egg mixture fill in under the cooked part. Continue until all the egg mixture is cooked. Carefully flip the omelet and cook for 30 seconds more.

3. Slide the omelet onto a plate and arrange the berries down the center. Fold both sides in to wrap the berries in the omelet, and turn the omelet over, so that the fold is on the bottom. Serve immediately.

Alice's Curious French Toast Bread Pudding

{ MAKES 8 SERVINGS }

FRENCH TOAST

6 eggs

1 cup heavy cream

1 cup sugar

1½ tablespoons pure vanilla extract

1 tablespoon freshly squeezed orange juice

1 tablespoon freshly squeezed lemon juice

1½ teaspoons ground cinnamon

1 loaf brioche (or challah, as a second choice), cut into eight ¾-inch-thick slices

Butter, for the pan

PUDDING BASE

¼ cup heavy cream

1 tablespoon Apricot Brandy tea leaves (see Resources)

4½ large egg yolks

Half of 1 large beaten egg

½ cup sugar

1½ tablespoons pure vanilla extract

WHEN WE DECIDED to start serving brunch, we were determined to stick with the original concept of the restaurant, "tea turned on its ear," so we racked our brains to come up with a way to do French toast that was unique, fun, and, most important, tasty! We all tossed a bunch of ideas out there, and one of them was French toast bread pudding. All heads tilted curiously at this idea, so of course we tried it. The idea was for it to be like a true bread pudding—tea-infused, of course—but when the first batch came out, our chef said, "I don't think this one is right—the top is crisp and chewy, but the bottom may be mushy." We tried it, and lo and behold, there it was, the brunch item that would make eyes widen and taste buds explode: a layer of crisp and chewy French toast on top and a wonderfully gooey, creamy bread pudding infused with apricot brandy tea underneath.

Note that you will need eight 2-inch-deep oven-safe glass bowls (8-ounce ramekins or crème brûlée dishes work well).

1. Preheat the oven to 350°F.

2. In a large mixing bowl, combine the eggs, heavy cream, sugar, vanilla extract, orange and lemon juices, and cinnamon. Whisk the mixture until it is smooth and combined, but do not overbeat it. Place each slice of bread into the mixture and let it absorb the liquid thoroughly. Set the soaked bread aside on a plate.

3. Place a griddle or a large frying pan over medium heat and coat it with butter. When the griddle is hot, cook each slice of bread until it is nicely golden on both sides, keeping the

(continued)

Pure maple syrup

Crème anglaise (recipe follows)

Fruit coulis (recipe follows)

Confectioners' sugar

Fresh fruit

heat at a level that allows the bread to cook through evenly without burning the egg mixture. As they are cooked, set the slices aside on a plate.

4. While the bread is cooking, make the pudding base: Bring the heavy cream to a simmer in a small saucepan, and then remove it from the heat. Place the tea leaves in a tea strainer and steep them in the cream for 3 minutes (or simply put the loose tea in the cream, steep for 3 minutes, and then strain carefully). Discard the tea leaves and reserve the Apricot Brandy cream.

5. In a medium bowl, combine the egg yolks, beaten egg, and sugar, and whisk to combine. Add a little of the egg mixture to the Apricot Brandy cream and continuing to whisk, gradually add the remaining egg mixture until it's fully combined. Stir in the vanilla extract. Set the pudding base aside.

6. When all the bread has been cooked on the griddle, cut the slices into 1 × 1-inch squares.

7. Pour the pudding base evenly into the eight ramekins (they will be about one-fourth full), and then lay in the bread squares (the bread may extend above the edge of the ramekins). Place the ramekins on a large baking sheet, and bake for 20 minutes, or until the bread is golden and crispy and the liquid is bubbling.

8. To serve, drizzle maple syrup, crème anglaise, fruit coulis, and/or confectioners' sugar on top—whatever your heart desires! Slices of fresh fruit work wonderfully as a garnish or a side. Be generous, whatever you do!

Dottie enjoying Alice's Curious French Toast Bread Pudding

FRUIT COULIS

2 cups strawberries, hulled

2 cups blueberries

2 cups blackberries

2 cups raspberries

1 cup sugar

In a large saucepan over low heat, cook the berries with 1 cup water until the mixture comes to a boil, stirring as needed. Add the sugar and stir until dissolved. Remove from the heat and set aside to cool. Puree the mixture in a blender, then strain (you will have to mash it through the strainer). Cover and refrigerate until ready to use.

CRÈME ANGLAISE

1 quart heavy cream

1 cup sugar

9 egg yolks

2 teaspoons vanilla extract

1. Set a large bowl in a bowl or pan of ice.

2. In a medium saucepan over low heat, lightly whisk together 2 cups (½ quart) of the heavy cream and the sugar until the sugar is incorporated (do not bring to a boil). Lightly whisk in the remaining 2 cups (½ quart) heavy cream and the egg yolks. Pour the mixture through a strainer, then return it to the saucepan and bring to a boil over high heat. Add the vanilla and mix gently with a spatula. When the vanilla is thoroughly incorporated, pour the mixture into the bowl over the ice so that it cools quickly. Cover and refrigerate for at least an hour.

3. You can prepare the crème anglaise in advance and store it for up to 5 days. Before using, stir or whisk again.

Alice's Pumpkin Pancakes

{ MAKES 16 TO 18 PANCAKES,
TO SERVE 4 }

2 teaspoons Orange Spice tea
leaves (see Resources)

2 cups all-purpose flour

½ cup sugar

2 teaspoons baking soda

1 tablespoon baking powder

1 teaspoon ground nutmeg

2¼ teaspoons ground cinnamon

1 teaspoon salt

2 cups buttermilk

¾ stick (6 tablespoons) unsalted
butter, melted, plus extra for
the pan and for serving

4 eggs, lightly beaten with a fork

2 cups canned pumpkin puree
(all pumpkin, not pumpkin pie
filling)

Pure maple syrup, for serving
(we prefer Grade B for its strong
maple flavor)

WE USED TO call these "pumpkin-filled pancakes," but people expected pumpkin to ooze out of them when they cut them. Not so. But we are generous with the pumpkin in this batter!

1. Put the tea leaves in a coffee or spice grinder, and grind until super-fine.

2. Place the ground tea, flour, sugar, baking soda, baking powder, nutmeg, cinnamon, and salt in a large mixing bowl and stir to combine.

3. One ingredient at a time, add the buttermilk, butter, eggs, and pumpkin to the dry mixture, mixing with a spatula until smooth after each addition (do not use a whisk). Let the batter sit for 15 minutes. Mix again with a spatula, and let it sit for 15 minutes more.

4. Place a large frying pan or a griddle over medium heat and add a little butter to the pan. When the butter is sizzling, use about half of a soup ladle of batter (or a ¼-cup measure) to make perfect-size pancakes. When bubbles start to burst on the top of the pancakes (after about 2 minutes), flip the pancakes and cook for about 2 minutes more, or until golden. As they finish cooking, place the pancakes on a baking sheet in a warm oven.

5. Serve with more butter and maple syrup!

"Alice's Tea" Sweet Crepes

{ MAKES 8 TO 10 CREPES,
TO SERVE 4 }

3 heaping teaspoons Alice's Tea leaves (see Resources)

1½ cups all-purpose flour

3 eggs

¾ cup whole milk

3 tablespoons unsalted butter, melted

¼ teaspoon kosher salt

Confectioners' sugar (for dusting)

WE USE OUR PROPRIETARY tea for this recipe because the green tea mixed with the rose petals mixed with the vanilla black tea of our Alice's Tea adds an elegant flavor to the batter, and we felt it was the perfect way to set "the crepe" apart from other worthy competitors. Fill or top these crepes with anything from mixed berries to lavender Earl Grey honey, mascarpone cheese, and figs (see the sidebar opposite). You could, in theory, eat nothing but these crepes and still have infinite variety! Crepes every day?! Hell, yeah . . .

1. Steep the tea leaves in 1 cup boiling-hot water for 3 minutes. Then strain the tea, cover it, and put it in the freezer for a few minutes to cool down rapidly.

2. In a large bowl, with a mixer set on the lowest speed, mix the flour and eggs together. With the mixer running, slowly pour in the milk and the cooled tea, and blend until well mixed. Turn the mixer up to medium speed, add the butter and salt, and mix until the batter is smooth.

3. Spray a frying pan or a griddle with nonstick cooking spray and set over medium heat. Using a soup ladle or a ½-cup measure, scoop out some batter and pour it into the pan. Tip the pan around in all directions to evenly distribute the batter (or use the back of a spoon to spread the batter in a large round on the griddle). Cook for about 1½ minutes, until set; then carefully flip the crepe with a spatula and cook for 1½ minutes on the other side. Set the crepes aside in a warm place as you finish with each one.

4. Place a crepe on a plate, put your favorite filling in a line down the center, and then roll it up. Repeat, give them all a dusting of confectioners' sugar, and enjoy!

Claire eating mixed berry crepes at Chapter I

Here are some of our favorite crepe fillings:

- ✦ Nutella and strawberries

- ✦ French Vervain Lemon Curd (page 171) and blackberries

- ✦ Mixed berries and chocolate sauce

- ✦ Caramel sauce and bananas

- ✦ Lavender Earl Grey–Infused Honey, mascarpone cheese, and figs

Lavender Earl Grey-Infused Honey

1 heaping teaspoon Lavender Earl Grey tea leaves (see Resources)

1 cup honey

Steep the Lavender Earl Grey tea leaves in ¼ cup boiling-hot water for 3 minutes. Strain the tea. In a small mixing bowl, combine the honey and 2 tablespoons of the tea, and stir until well mixed. Store, covered, in the refrigerator until ready to use—it will keep for about 2 weeks. We also recommend using it in tea, or with cheeses and fruit!

Wonderland Waffles

{ MAKES 8 TO 10 WAFFLES,
TO SERVE 4 }

2 cups half-and-half

½ teaspoon Mauritius tea leaves
(see Resources)

2 cups all-purpose flour

2 tablespoons sugar

1 tablespoon baking powder

1 stick (½ cup) unsalted butter,
melted

4 eggs

✦ Tip ✦

Tea is a spice! Experiment
by using brewed tea in your
marinades and other
cooking and baking liquids,
and by grinding dry tea
leaves in a coffee or spice
grinder and adding them
directly to your food.

LIGHT AND FLUFFY, these waffles have a ton of flavor on their own but also shine in the presence of sweet stuff or simply some mixed berries. The Mauritius tea–infused batter sets them apart.

1. In a small saucepan over low heat, heat the half-and-half and Mauritius tea leaves until the liquid turns medium brown, 7 to 10 minutes. Using an all-cotton tea filter sock (or a cheese cloth–lined strainer) strain the tea leaves out of the half-and-half. Set the half-and-half mixture aside and discard the tea leaves.

2. Combine the flour, sugar, and baking powder in a large mixing bowl. Add the butter, eggs, and half-and-half mixture and whisk until smooth.

3. Heat a waffle iron to 3.5, or the medium setting, and use a soup ladle or a ½-cup measure to pour the mixture into the waffle iron. Cook each waffle for 2 to 3 minutes, or until golden. As they finish cooking, place the waffles on a baking sheet in a warm oven.

Alice's Vanilla Tea–Infused Granola

{ MAKES ABOUT 7 CUPS,
OR 14 SERVINGS }

2½ cups rolled oats

½ cup chopped walnuts

½ cup chopped almonds

½ cup chopped pecans

¾ cup sweetened shredded coconut

¼ cup sesame seeds

2 heaping teaspoons Vanilla
tea leaves (see Resources),
finely ground in a coffee or
spice grinder

1 tablespoon ground cinnamon

⅛ teaspoon ground nutmeg

¼ teaspoon kosher salt

½ cup sliced dried apricots

½ cup dried cranberries or cherries

⅓ cup honey, plus more for
drizzling

½ stick (¼ cup) unsalted butter,
melted

THIS HAS QUICKLY become our most popular breakfast item, and for good reason! It's not a muesli-style granola—we mix our granola with vanilla tea, drizzle it with honey, and bake it until it's good and toasty. Then we break it into pieces, but just barely—so that you can break it further with your spoon or pick it up like a granola bar.

1. Preheat the oven to 350°F, and spray a large baking sheet with cooking spray.

2. In a large bowl, combine all the ingredients *except* the honey and butter, and mix thoroughly. Then stir in the honey and butter.

3. Spread the mixture evenly on the prepared baking sheet, and pack it down with the back of a spatula. Bake the granola until the top is golden brown, about 10 minutes.

4. Remove the baking sheet from the oven and use a large spatula to flip the granola over. Pack the granola down with the spatula and drizzle a little honey on top. Bake for 10 minutes, or until the granola is nice and brown and crunchy. Set the granola aside to cool completely.

5. Break the cooked granola into chunks and larger pieces. Store in an airtight container in a cool, dry place so that the granola doesn't get soggy and make you sad . . .

6. Enjoy with milk or yogurt, or just eat it by itself as a yummy snack!

Soups and Salads

✦ ✦ ✦

SOUPS

On a cold day, there's nothing like warming yourself up with a bowl of soup. And in the summer, when you're either too hot from being outside or too cold from sitting in a blast of air-conditioning, soup provides the perfect, well-balanced meal. Soups can be purees that are comforting to sip off your spoon or heartier fare that convinces you that you won't ever need to eat again. Whatever your preference, we have a wonderful and unique soup for you.

A while back, Lauren discovered the magical slow cooker—and her life has never been the same. In fact, the slow cooker would be near the top of her list of items for a desert island (assuming the island had electricity). If you don't own a slow cooker, considering buying one, as making soups (and rice and a whole host of other things) becomes so much easier—and if you make enough at one time, you'll have ready-to-heat meals for the rest of the week!

✦ Tip ✦
When you put a pot of soup in the fridge overnight and plan to reheat it the next day, put a whole (clean!) potato in the soup. The potato will absorb some of the salt, preventing the soup from tasting too salty when it's reheated, which happens naturally through evaporation while cooking.

Ryan pouring a cup of tea for Celeste Holm at Chapter III

Turkey Chili

{ MAKES 8 TO 10 SERVINGS }

½ stick (4 tablespoons) butter

3 pounds ground turkey

Kosher salt and freshly ground
    black pepper

1 cup finely chopped carrots
    (about 2 medium carrots)

½ cup finely chopped red onion
    (about ½ medium onion)

½ cup finely chopped celery
    (about 1 large stalk)

2 garlic cloves, minced

2½ cups unseasoned tomato sauce
    (from two and a half 8-ounce
    cans)

1½ cups chopped tomatoes
    (from one 13.5-ounce can; we
    recommend Muir Glen), drained

One 15.5-ounce can black beans,
    drained

One 15.5-ounce can navy beans,
    drained

One 15.5-ounce can kidney beans,
    drained

1½ teaspoons chili powder

1 teaspoon ground cumin

THIS IS A CULT favorite of ours that started as a special and became a daily staple. With fresh ground turkey, three types of beans, tomatoes, and our special blend of spices, this hearty bowl of flavorful goodness is the perfect meal.

1. Melt 2 tablespoons of the butter in a skillet over medium heat. Add the ground turkey and sauté until it is lightly browned, but not burned, 3 to 5 minutes. Add salt and pepper to taste, and set the turkey aside.

2. Melt the remaining 2 tablespoons butter in a large soup pot or Dutch oven, and sauté the carrots, onions, celery, and garlic until softened, 8 to 10 minutes (take care not to burn them).

3. Add the tomato sauce and chopped tomatoes, bring to a simmer, and cook for 10 minutes. Add the black, navy, and kidney beans to the pot, and simmer for another 10 minutes. Add the turkey and cook for 15 minutes. Add the chili powder, cumin, and salt and pepper to taste, and simmer for 10 minutes.

Slow cooker instructions: After you've browned the turkey and sautéed the vegetables, throw everything into a slow cooker, set the heat to low, and cook for 3 to 4 hours—it will make your home smell like heaven!

Rooibos Tomato Soup

{ MAKES 8 TO 10 SERVINGS }

½ cup plus 2 teaspoons extra-
   virgin olive oil

½ cup chopped celery (about
   1 large stalk)

½ cup chopped red onion (about
   1 medium onion)

2 garlic cloves, chopped

8 cups good-quality vegetable stock
   (we recommend Imagine brand)

3 tablespoons Organic Rooibos tea
   leaves (see Resources)

7 cups canned chopped tomatoes
   (from four 13.5-ounce cans;
   we recommend Muir Glen)

3 bay leaves

Kosher salt and freshly ground
   black pepper

WE USED TO BE regulars at Chado, a wonderful little teahouse in West Hollywood where the tomato soup was out of this world. It was delicious—not too acidic, not too sweet, just the perfect tomato soup. Well, we worked and worked to make one of our own that incorporated all the great things we remembered about theirs, plus an organic Rooibos tea infusion . . .

1. Heat 2 teaspoons of the olive oil in a medium sauté pan over medium heat. Add the celery, onions, and garlic, and sauté until slightly tender, 7 to 10 minutes.

2. Meanwhile, combine about ½ cup of the vegetable stock and the tea leaves in a small saucepan over medium heat, and heat to just boiling. Remove the pan from the heat and let it stand for 5 minutes to steep. Then strain the stock, saving the stock and discarding the tea leaves.

3. Combine the sautéed vegetables, the tea-infused stock, the remaining 7½ cups stock, the tomatoes, and the bay leaves in a large soup pot or Dutch oven. Cover, and cook over medium heat for 1 hour.

4. Remove the pot from the heat, remove the bay leaves (don't forget this step!), and pour the mixture into a blender or a food processor, working in batches if necessary. Puree the mixture, slowly drizzling in the remaining ½ cup olive oil while the machine is running, until the soup is fully blended and the consistency is creamy. Add salt and pepper to taste. Voilà—soup!

5. This soup is terrific served with one of our savory scones—we choose Walnut Stilton!

(continued)

Slow cooker instructions: Place all the ingredients, *except* the ½ cup olive oil and the salt and pepper, in a slow cooker, set the heat to medium, and cook for 2 to 4 hours. When the soup is fully cooked and the house smells divine, remove the bay leaves and puree as described, adding the oil and seasoning with salt and pepper.

✦   ✦   ✦

Apple-Cinnamon Butternut Squash Soup

{ MAKES 8 TO 10 SERVINGS }

2 medium butternut squash

1 stick (½ cup) unsalted butter, melted

½ cup chopped red onion (about 1 medium onion)

8 cups good-quality chicken stock (we recommend Imagine brand)

2 rounded tablespoons Cinnamon Apple Spice tea leaves (see Resources)

Kosher salt and freshly ground black pepper

ÜBER-CREAMY IN TEXTURE but cream-free—yes! (It would be dairy-free except that we use butter to roast the squash.) The cinnamon apple spice tea infusion adds a kick. We use chicken stock for added flavor, but you could substitute vegetable stock to make it vegetarian—it's great either way!

1. Preheat the oven to 400°F, and spray a large baking sheet with cooking spray.

2. Stem the squash, cut them in half lengthwise, and scrape out the pulp and seeds, discarding them. Cut the halves in half lengthwise (to make quarters), and lay them skin side down on the prepared baking sheet. Use a pastry brush to paint the cut surfaces with the butter, reserving any extra butter. Cover the squash with aluminum foil and roast for 1 hour, or until they are tender.

3. Meanwhile, heat a bit of the remaining butter in a small sauté pan over low heat. Add the onions and sauté until they are just tender, about 3 minutes (take care not to burn them). Set the onions aside.

4. In a small saucepan over low heat, bring ½ cup of the chicken stock and the tea leaves just to a boil. Strain, and reserve the stock, discarding the tea leaves.

5. Use a paring knife to cut the skin from the cooked squash (the skin should come off easily), and cut the squash into cubes.

6. Combine the squash, sautéed onions, infused stock, and remaining 7½ cups stock in a large soup pot or Dutch oven. Cover, and cook over medium heat for 45 to 60 minutes, or until the squash falls apart when you stick a fork through it.

7. Carefully ladle the soup into a blender or a food processor, in batches if necessary, and puree until smooth. Then add salt and pepper to taste, and serve.

Slow cooker instructions: Place the uncooked squash (cut into pieces and peeled), the sautéed onions, and the rest of the ingredients (except the salt and pepper) in a slow cooker set to low heat, and cook for 3 to 6 hours. Puree and season as described.

The service bar at Chapter II

Green Goddess Soup

{ MAKES 8 TO 10 SERVINGS }

2 tablespoons unsalted butter

½ cup chopped yellow onion

½ small celery stalk, chopped

3 garlic cloves, chopped

20 to 30 asparagus spears, bottom
    ends removed

1 large handful fresh watercress

One 5-ounce bag fresh spinach

8 cups chicken stock (we
    recommend Imagine brand)

Kosher salt and freshly ground
    black pepper

PEOPLE ALWAYS ASK, "What is in this soup?" because they can't believe that a soup this healthy can taste so good! It's truly a simple soup to make, chock-full of green veggies that are cooked and pureed with some chicken stock (vegetable stock works really well, too, for all the vegetarians out there). Even kids will eat this soup—it has *that* much good flavor! If, like us, you love sopping up a flavorful soup with some bread, try some absorbent focaccia.

1. Heat the butter in a medium sauté pan over low heat. Add the onions, celery, and garlic, and sauté until the vegetables have softened, about 5 minutes (take care not to burn them).

2. Combine the sautéed vegetables, asparagus, watercress, spinach, and stock in a large soup pot or Dutch oven. Cover, and cook over medium heat for 1 hour.

3. Carefully ladle the soup into a blender or a food processor, in batches if necessary, and puree until smooth. Then add salt and pepper to taste, and serve.

Slow cooker instructions: Place the sautéed vegetables and the rest of the ingredients (except the salt and pepper) in a slow cooker set to low heat, and cook for 3 to 6 hours. Puree and season as described.

Thai Chickpea Soup

{ MAKES 8 TO 10 SERVINGS }

2 tablespoons unsalted butter

¼ cup minced jalapeño pepper

½ cup chopped celery (1 medium stalk)

¾ cup chopped yellow onion (1 medium to large onion)

8 cups good-quality chicken stock (we recommend Imagine brand)

One 13.5-ounce can coconut milk

One 13.5-ounce can crushed tomatoes (we recommend Muir Glen)

¼ cup freshly squeezed lime juice

Two 13.5-ounce cans chickpeas, drained

Kosher salt and freshly ground black pepper

THIS IS ON THE spicy side, with jalapeños (note: wash your hands after cutting the jalapeños before you, say, accidentally rub your eyes—we warn from experience). So if you want it less spicy, dial down the jalapeños. But if you *do* like it hot, add some more to this coconutty soup.

We find this to be a great alternative to chicken soup when you have a cold. The spiciness really helps with congestion!

1. Heat the butter in a medium sauté pan over low heat. Add the jalapeños, celery, and onions, and sauté until the vegetables have softened, about 5 minutes (take care not to burn them).

2. Combine the vegetables with the stock, coconut milk, tomatoes, and lime juice in a large soup pot or Dutch oven. Cover, and cook over medium heat for 45 to 60 minutes.

3. Add the chickpeas and cook for 5 minutes, or until they are heated through. Add salt and pepper to taste, and serve.

We are serious carb fiends (case in point: this cookbook), but we were raised on salads. I mean, we did eat a lot of other things, but we *always* had salad with dinner: Mom's rule. We have her mantra "Eat a green!" burned into our brains. She clearly wasn't hip to the salad-as-a-meal thing then . . . or maybe, like most moms, she felt it necessary to fill us with complex carbs before bed each night and didn't know how to infiltrate her pure salads with such fare. But when we were thinking about salads for Alice's, we decided that we wanted them to act as a meal, full of good proteins and sometimes rich components, so that the result would be fresh, filling, and unexpectedly pleasing.

Lapsang Souchong Smoked Chicken Salad

{ MAKES 4 SERVINGS }

4 large handfuls mixed field greens

4 Lapsang Souchong Smoked Chicken breasts (page 78), cut lengthwise into ¼-inch-thick slices

2 Granny Smith Apples, cored and cut into ¼-inch-thick slices

4 Maté Carnival tea–soaked eggs (see page 80, steps 1 through 3), quartered

1 cup shredded carrots

1 cup Alice's House Dressing (recipe follows)

OUR MOST POPULAR salad at all locations, this is as delicious as it is healthy! We use all the components of its sister sandwich (page 76), minus the herbed goat cheese spread, and pile them on top of a mound of mixed field greens, along with wedges of our Maté Carnival tea–soaked eggs and a drizzle of Alice's House Dressing. Our father, Ray, tells us that even if we didn't own Alice's, he'd come every week for this salad. Imagine, something delicious that's good for you, too . . .

Note: The chicken takes at least 2 days to marinate, so plan in advance.

1. Place the greens on a dinner plate. Fan the sliced chicken over one side of the salad and the apple slices over the other side. Arrange the egg quarters around the salad, and place the shredded carrots in a mound where there is room between the chicken and apple slices.

2. Drizzle with Alice's House Dressing, or serve the dressing on the side.

ALICE'S HOUSE DRESSING

{ MAKES 1½ CUPS }

CONCENTRATE

5 medium shallots

1½ teaspoons olive oil

2 garlic cloves, minced

1 tablespoon minced fresh ginger

3½ cups soy sauce

2½ cups balsamic vinegar

2½ cups rice vinegar

¾ cup molasses

½ cup freshly squeezed orange juice

¼ cup freshly squeezed lemon juice

5 tablespoons honey

½ cup firmly packed dark
brown sugar

DRESSING

1¼ cups Alice's House Dressing
Concentrate (above)

2 tablespoons Dijon mustard

2 cups canola oil

Salt and pepper

People love our house dressing and are constantly asking for the recipe. Well, here it is! Sure, there are a lot of ingredients and it takes some time, but it's so worth it. You start by cooking down a concentrate with a bunch of wonderful flavors, then emulsify it with oil and Dijon mustard. Delicious!

1. *To prepare the concentrate:* Preheat the oven to 400°F. Toss the shallots in 1 teaspoon of the olive oil, and lay them on a baking sheet. Roast them in the oven for 50 minutes, or until nicely tender and browned. Cut the shallots into ½-inch-thick slices.

2. Heat the remaining ½ teaspoon olive oil in a large pot or Dutch oven over low heat. Add the roasted shallots, garlic, and ginger, and sauté until caramelized, 8 to 10 minutes—do not burn! Add all the remaining concentrate ingredients, bring to a boil, and cook for 30 minutes.

3. Reduce the heat to low and simmer for 2 hours, or until thickened and reduced.

4. Refrigerate unused concentrate for up to 2 weeks.

5. *To make the dressing:* Add the concentrate and the mustard to a food processor or a blender, and turn it on. With the motor running, slowly drizzle in the oil, blending until the dressing has emulsified. Adjust the seasonings as desired, and serve.

Warm Lentil Salad

{ MAKES 4 SERVINGS }

2 cups French green lentils

1 small onion

*2 carrots: 1 cut into 3 chunks,
1 cut into ¼-inch dice (about
⅔ cup dice)*

*2 celery stalks: 1 cut into 3 chunks,
1 cut into ¼-inch dice (about
⅔ cup dice)*

Kosher or sea salt

4 bacon strips (optional)

*2 tablespoons extra-virgin olive oil
(plus 2 more tablespoons if not
using bacon)*

Freshly ground black pepper

2 tablespoons balsamic vinegar

*4 teaspoons freshly squeezed
lemon juice*

½ teaspoon honey

*4 large handfuls mixed
field greens*

THIS SALAD HAS been on our menu since our first restaurant opened. Marc Cohn, who lived near our flagship location, would order it "to go" for lunch several times a week. Back then we were still experimenting a lot with the menu, and for some insane reason we took it off the menu after a few months. One day we came in and were handed a note that read, "Marc Cohn wants you to know that he is very sad that the lentil salad is no longer on the menu and thinks you should reconsider." Well, we sure did, and we're so glad we listened to Mr. Cohn, because it's a customer favorite—French lentils sautéed with bacon and served atop mixed field greens. If you see Marc Cohn, thank him for us!

Note: The salad can be made with or without bacon—your choice.

1. Place the lentils, whole onion, carrot and celery chunks, and 3 cups water in a pot and bring to a boil. Then reduce the heat to low and cook until the lentils are just about tender, 35 to 40 minutes—do not overcook!

2. Discard the onion, carrots, and celery. Drain the lentils and run cold water over them to stop the cooking. Place the lentils in a large mixing bowl, season them well with salt, and set aside.

3. If you're using the bacon, fry it in a sauté pan over medium heat until it's crisp, not chewy—but don't burn it! Set the bacon aside on a paper towel to absorb the fat. Keep 2 tablespoons of the bacon fat in the pan, and discard the rest (or put it in a glass jar in the fridge for use in other recipes).

4. Add the diced carrots and celery to the sauté pan (along with 2 tablespoons olive oil if you're not using bacon), and sauté until they are just tender, 5 to 7 minutes. Add a pinch of salt and pepper, and set aside.

5. In a large mixing bowl, combine the lentils, the sautéed carrots and celery, the 2 tablespoons olive oil, and the balsamic vinegar, lemon juice, and honey. Crumble the bacon strips, if using, into the bowl. Mix well, and add salt and pepper to taste. Serve warm over a bed of mixed field greens.

Golden Afternoon Salad

{ MAKES 6 TO 8 SERVINGS }

4 medium red beets

4 medium yellow beets

½ cup orzo

Kosher salt and freshly ground
    black pepper

1½ teaspoons canola oil

1 garlic clove, chopped

3 tablespoons red wine vinegar

2 carrots, cut into ½-inch dice

1 cup canned whole baby corn

¼ teaspoon minced fresh tarragon

¼ teaspoon minced fresh chives

¼ teaspoon minced fresh thyme

¼ teaspoon minced fresh chervil

1 tablespoon goat cheese

2 teaspoons whole milk

6 ounces mixed field greens

WE LOVE BEETS, but the standard problem in a beet salad is that beet juice is so potent and colorful that it's hard to keep the colors separate. We decided to embrace the juice and go for a pink salad—it's such a fun surprise, maybe you can get your kids to eat it! Packed with creamy goat cheese and other vegetables and herbs in addition to the beets, this delicious salad is full of protein, healthy fats, vitamins, and nutrients.

1. Place all the beets in a medium saucepan and pour in enough water to cover them. Bring the water to a boil over medium heat, and cook until the beets are tender, 20 to 30 minutes. Drain the beets and set them aside to cool.

2. Peel the cooled beets (the skins will slip off easily), and cut them into 1-inch chunks. Set them aside.

3. Bring a small saucepan of water to a boil over low heat. Add the orzo, a pinch of salt, a pinch of pepper, and ½ teaspoon of the oil, and simmer until al dente, 8 to 10 minutes. Drain and set aside.

4. Heat the remaining 1 teaspoon oil in a medium sauté pan over medium heat. Add the garlic and sauté until browned. Then add the vinegar and 1 teaspoon water, and stir briefly to emulsify the liquids. Add the beets, carrots, baby corn, and a pinch of salt and pepper. Sauté for 3 to 5 minutes, but don't overcook—the carrots and baby corn are best with a bit of crunch to them. Set aside.

5. In a large bowl, combine the herbs, goat cheese, and milk, and stir to blend. Add the orzo and the sautéed vegetables, and mix carefully to incorporate all the ingredients.

6. Divide the greens among the desired number of plates, top with the beet mixture, and serve.

Warm Pear and Endive Salad

{ MAKES 4 SERVINGS }

4 Anjou pears

1 tablespoon freshly squeezed lemon juice

3 tablespoons butter, melted

Kosher salt and freshly ground black pepper

½ cup Alice's Pear Dressing (recipe follows)

3 Belgian endive heads, cut across into ½-inch-wide slices

1 small red onion, cut in half lengthwise, then cut into ½-inch-thick slices

4 large handfuls fresh watercress

½ cup crumbled Stilton cheese

A MAJOR FAVORITE at Alice's, this warm salad has been described as "like eating a steak salad, but without any meat in it." In fact, this hearty salad would be wonderful served alongside a juicy steak. The sourness of the balsamic vinegar mixed with the sweetness of the sautéed pears is a delight!

1. Preheat the oven to 350°F.

2. Core the pears, then cut them into ¼-inch dice, leaving the skin on. As you cut them, place them in a bowl of cold water to prevent them from oxidizing. Then drain the pears and toss them in a bowl with the lemon juice, butter, and salt and pepper to taste. Spread the pears on a baking sheet and roast until just slightly tender, 10 to 12 minutes. Set the pears aside to cool on the baking sheet.

3. Heat ¼ cup of the pear dressing in a medium sauté pan over medium heat. Add the endive and onions, and sauté until they are slightly tender, 3 to 5 minutes. Add the pears and sauté for another 2 minutes, adding salt and pepper to taste. Remove from the heat.

4. For each serving, place a handful of watercress on a plate and top with a portion of the warm sautéed endive, onions, and pears. Sprinkle each salad with 2 tablespoons of the cheese. Then drizzle a tablespoon of Alice's Pear Dressing on top, and serve right away!

ALICE'S PEAR DRESSING

{ MAKES 1½ CUPS }

CONCENTRATE

1 teaspoon unsalted butter

¾ teaspoon canola oil

2 Anjou pears, cored and cubed

½ cup port wine

½ cup balsamic vinegar

½ cup white wine vinegar

DRESSING

1¼ cups Alice's Pear Dressing
   Concentrate (above)

2 tablespoons Dijon mustard

2 cups canola oil

Salt and pepper

1. *To prepare the concentrate:* Heat the butter and oil in a medium saucepan over low to medium heat. Add the pears and sauté for 15 minutes, or until softened. Add the port and the vinegars, and simmer over low heat until the pears are soft enough to puree, 15 to 20 minutes.

2. *To make the dressing:* Add the concentrate and mustard to a food processor or a blender, and turn it on. With the motor running, slowly drizzle in the oil, blending until the dressing has emulsified. Adjust the seasonings as desired, and serve. (Store extra dressing in an airtight container in the refrigerator for up to 2 weeks.)

Alice's Steak Salad

{ MAKES 1 SERVING }

3 tablespoons canola oil

1 teaspoon minced fresh thyme

1 teaspoon minced fresh rosemary

1 garlic clove, minced

1 pinch kosher salt

1 pinch freshly ground black pepper

*1 medium boneless strip steak
  (10 to 12 ounces)*

1 teaspoon butter

*3 bacon strips, cut into ½-inch
  pieces*

1 handful mixed field greens

½ tomato, cubed

½ cucumber, cubed

*1 Maté Carnival tea–soaked egg
  (see page 80, steps 1 through 3),
  quartered*

*½ Granny Smith apple, cored
  and cubed*

¼ cup herbed croutons

*¼ cup sweet chili sauce (we like
  Mae Ploy brand)*

THE STEAK FOR this salad is prepared very simply—but plan ahead, because it marinates for two days. When you combine it with apples, eggs, and bacon and top the salad with a sweet chili sauce, there's magic on the plate!

1. In a medium bowl or a zip-top storage bag, combine the oil, herbs, garlic, and salt and pepper. Add the steak, turn to coat it thoroughly, cover or seal, and refrigerate for 2 days.

2. On a grill or in a very hot skillet, cook the steak to your liking (we recommend medium-rare). Let the steak rest for 10 minutes after cooking.

3. Melt the butter in a skillet over medium heat, and cook the bacon until it is slightly crispy, about 5 minutes—do not burn it. Set the bacon aside on paper towels to drain.

4. Use a sharp knife to cut the steak on the diagonal into 1-inch-thick strips.

5. Put the greens in a heaping pile on a dinner plate, and fan the steak strips around the greens. Fill the gaps between the bottoms of the steak strips with the tomatoes, cucumbers, bacon, egg wedges, apples, and croutons.

6. Serve with the sweet chili sauce on the side so that the spiciness and sweetness can be controlled.

Sandwiches

✦ ✦ ✦

Most of us eat sandwiches because we got used to them when we were little—sandwiches in our packed lunches, sandwiches to eat on the fly, sandwiches to be thrown together in five minutes or less. But how often have we given thought to how we actually feel about those sandwiches?

Sandwiches are too easy not to eat, but as with the common scone, we tend to rely on them to fill us up rather than make them into something special. When you see a menu full of sandwiches, often you'll want some of the components but not all of them—oh, the eternal struggle to choose and enjoy a sandwich!

The more tearooms we visited, the more we started questioning the standard tea sandwiches. Why only mayonnaise and turkey? Why butter and cucumber alone? Why white bread? Why not cut a sandwich into thirds instead of two pieces? Why, why, why?

Sandwiches should be put together with forethought, considering all the components, dissecting the ingredients, and examining what flavors might boost other flavors. For example, we're in love with the golden raisin fennel semolina bread from Amy's Bread in New York City because it completes our croque monsieur, making what is already a wonderful sandwich an incredible one. Simply adding chives and lemon zest to the butter for our cucumber sandwich, and using an earthy wheat bread, turns it from ordinary to extraordinary. Read on to find the stories (and recipes!) behind some of our favorite sandwiches—and feel inspired to concoct your own perfect combinations. Life's too short to settle for a sad sandwich.

Lapsang Souchong Smoked Chicken Sandwiches

{ MAKES 8 SANDWICHES }

16 slices 7-grain or other whole-grain bread

1 cup Herbed Goat Cheese Spread (recipe follows)

1 Granny Smith apple

1 cup mesclun greens

32 to 48 thin slices Lapsang Souchong Smoked Chicken (recipe follows)

WE HAD TRIED a chicken sandwich at a teahouse in Los Angeles that had lingonberries in it and we loved the combination of the salty, savory chicken and the tart, sweet berries, so we challenged our chef to come up with our own sweet/savory version. Of course we wanted to incorporate our favorite concept—tea! Instead of infusing a spread with tea or just using it to marinate the chicken, we decided to take it a step further and smoke the chicken with tea, too. (Well, technically it's steamed, but the water cooks off quickly, and cooking the chicken with the tea gives it a definite smoky effect.) We chose Lapsang Souchong because, as those in the know know, it's *very* smoky. Our first bite into this sandwich made us downright giddy. The sweet-and-sour Granny Smith apple combined with the tea-smoked chicken breast was exactly what we had in mind.

NOTE: The chicken in this recipe is marinated for 2 or 3 days, so plan in advance—it's worth the effort!

1. Lay 8 slices of the bread on a clean counter and spread about 1 tablespoon of the goat cheese spread on each slice. Core the apple (but do not peel it), quarter it, and cut each quarter into 6 thin slices. Place 3 apple slices on each slice of bread, covering the goat cheese spread completely if possible. Place a few mesclun leaves on top of the apple slices, so that the apples are covered. Finally, place 4 to 6 slices of chicken (about 4 ounces) on top of the greens, and cover each sandwich with a second slice of bread.

2. Slice the sandwiches in half to serve, or if you want to serve finger sandwiches on an afternoon tea stand, cut off the crusts and cut each sandwich into 3 strips. Enjoy!

HERBED GOAT CHEESE SPREAD

{ MAKES ABOUT 1 CUP }

1 small unpeeled garlic clove

Olive oil, for brushing the garlic

8 ounces goat cheese (chèvre)

2 tablespoons cream cheese

¾ teaspoon dried tarragon

¾ teaspoon dried chervil

¾ teaspoon minced fresh chives

¾ teaspoon minced fresh thyme

1 tiny pinch salt

1 tiny pinch freshly ground black pepper

1. Preheat the oven or a toaster oven to 350°F.

2. Brush the garlic clove with olive oil, place it on a small ovenproof dish, and roast it for 10 to 15 minutes, or until it is soft. Peel the garlic. (Feel free to make extra roast garlic for other purposes—it's incredibly handy!)

3. Place the goat cheese, cream cheese, tarragon, chervil, chives, thyme, salt, and pepper in a mixer or a food processor and process until creamy. Add the roasted garlic and process until incorporated. If the spread is too thick, add a few drops of whole milk. (The spread will keep for about a week, covered, in the refrigerator.)

LAPSANG SOUCHONG SMOKED CHICKEN

{ MAKES 1½ CUPS }

MARINADE

2 tablespoons Lapsang Souchong Superior tea leaves (see Resources)

¾ cup soy sauce

¼ cup plus 2 tablespoons balsamic vinegar

¼ cup orange juice, preferably freshly squeezed

¼ cup lemon juice, preferably freshly squeezed

2 small garlic cloves, halved

1½ teaspoons ground ginger

4 teaspoons firmly packed dark brown sugar

½ teaspoon kosher salt

½ teaspoon freshly ground black pepper

Don't worry about making too much chicken—it's also delicious in our Lapsang Souchong Smoked Chicken Salad (page 63).

1. At least 2 days in advance of cooking the chicken, prepare the marinade: Combine ½ cup boiling-hot water and the Lapsang Souchong Superior tea leaves in a small bowl, and steep for 3 minutes. Then strain the tea, discarding the tea leaves. Set the tea aside.

2. In a plastic or glass container that's large enough to hold the chicken breasts, combine all the remaining marinade ingredients. Add 2 cups cold water and the reserved tea. Stir well. Place the chicken in the marinade, cover, and marinate for 2 or even 3 days in the refrigerator.

3. When you are ready to cook the chicken, preheat the oven to 350°F.

4. Set a perforated steamer tray over a pan containing ½ cup water and the ¼ cup plus 2 tablespoons Lapsang Souchong Superior tea leaves.

5. Combine the five-spice powder, salt, and pepper, and sprinkle the mixture generously over each chicken breast. Use your clean hands to rub the mixture thoroughly over the entire surface of the chicken; don't worry about overseasoning! Lay the chicken in the steamer tray, making sure it doesn't touch the water, and place the pan in the oven. Cook the chicken for 40 minutes (add 5 minutes for extra-large chicken breasts).

CHICKEN

3 boneless, skinless chicken breasts, any fat removed

¼ cup plus 2 tablespoons Lapsang Souchong Superior tea leaves (see Resources)

2 tablespoons Chinese five-spice powder

1 teaspoon kosher salt

1 teaspoon freshly ground black pepper

6. Use tongs to flip the breasts over, and turn the pan from front to back in the oven (this will ensure even cooking). Cook for 10 minutes. Then use a meat thermometer to test the temperature of the chicken (go in from the side of a breast so that you can reach the center): it should reach (but not exceed) 160°F. When the chicken is fully cooked, set it aside to cool for 20 minutes.

7. Use a very sharp knife to cut each breast lengthwise into ⅛-inch-thick slices. (If you are going to use any of the chicken for the chicken salad on page 63, you'll want to make thicker slices.) Make sure the chicken is cooked throughout. If it's not fully cooked, place it back in the steamer for a few more minutes—but don't overcook it, or your chicken will be too dry! Store, covered, in the refrigerator for up to 5 days.

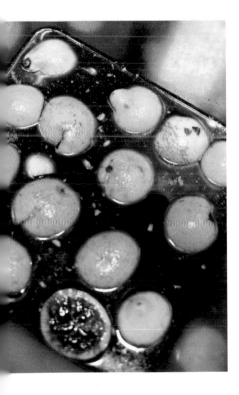

Our Lapsang marinade being prepped

Maté Carnival Egg Salad Sandwiches

{ MAKES 3 SANDWICHES }

2 tablespoons Maté Carnival tea leaves (see Resources)

4 eggs

1 teaspoon minced fresh chervil

1 teaspoon minced fresh thyme

1 teaspoon minced fresh chives

1 teaspoon minced fresh tarragon

1 teaspoon freshly squeezed lemon juice

2 pinches salt, plus more to taste

½ teaspoon freshly ground black pepper, plus more to taste

2 tablespoons mayonnaise (we prefer Hellmann's), plus more for spreading

6 slices 7-grain bread

1 cup mesclun greens

WHEN WE STARTED THINKING about egg salad, we decided it would be fun to soak the hard-boiled eggs in tea. We wanted a black tea for flavor—something strong and bold. Maté Carnival! Done and done. So we soaked the eggs, we made the salad, and we looked at it with trepidation. Hmm. Frankly, it was a rather odd brown color. But when we bravely ventured to taste it, we couldn't believe how good it was! We decided to serve it and see . . . and guess what? No one said anything about the brownish hue. In fact, no one even seemed to notice—they were too busy eating it up!

1. Steep the tea leaves in 2 cups boiling-hot water for 3 minutes (a little longer if you want a stronger tea flavor to the eggs). Strain the tea, discarding the tea leaves, and set the tea aside to cool to room temperature.

2. While the tea is cooling, hard-boil the eggs: Bring a small saucepan of water to a boil, add the eggs, and cook for 9 minutes. Drain the eggs and set them aside to cool.

3. When both the tea and the eggs have cooled, peel the eggs and place them in the tea, making sure they are fully covered. Soak the eggs in the tea for 1 to 1½ hours at room temperature; then drain the eggs and discard the tea.

4. In a medium bowl, mix the chervil, thyme, chives, tarragon, lemon juice, salt, and pepper. Slice the eggs in half and separate the whites from the yolks. In a food processor, pulse the egg whites into small cubes (do *not* puree), or simply cube the whites by hand. Add the whites to the herb mixture.

5. In a small bowl, carefully blend 3 of the egg yolks with the mayonnaise to make a smooth paste. (Reserve the fourth yolk.) Add the egg yolk mixture to the egg white mixture, and carefully mix by hand. Taste the egg salad, and add salt and pepper to taste. If the mixture needs to be thicker, break up the fourth yolk and mix it into the egg salad.

6. Spread the egg salad on 3 slices of bread, and top with some of the greens. Spread a little mayonnaise on the other 3 slices of bread, top the sandwiches with the bread, and *voilà!*

Cumin Carrot Sandwich

{ MAKES 1 SANDWICH }

2 slices black seed semolina bread

1 tablespoon Herbed Goat Cheese Spread (page 77)

1 tablespoon Olive Tapenade (recipe follows)

10 to 12 slices Roasted Cumin Carrots (page 84)

1 handful mixed field greens

OLIVE TAPENADE

{ MAKES 1½ CUPS }

2 cups mixed pitted black and green olives

1 tablespoon minced fresh tarragon

1 tablespoon minced fresh chives

1 tablespoon minced fresh chervil

1 tablespoon minced fresh thyme

1 tablespoon minced fresh rosemary

¼ cup sour cream

1½ teaspoons honey

1 pinch kosher salt

1 pinch freshly ground black pepper

WHEN THE CONCEPT FOR this sandwich was first presented to us, quite honestly, we tilted our heads in utter confusion: a carrot sandwich? Really? Really. But we tried it, and it absolutely dazzled us with its complex flavor layers: thinly sliced, cumin-rubbed roasted carrots, olive tapenade, herbed goat cheese, and greens between slices of black seed semolina bread. Be sure to slice the carrots really thin and get a good brown on them in the roasting process . . . they're great on salads as well as in this sandwich!

1. Spread 1 slice of bread with the goat cheese spread and the other slice with the olive tapenade.

2. Layer the carrot slices across the tapenade, folding them to give the sandwich volume. Top the carrots with the greens and place the goat cheese–covered bread on top. Cut the sandwich in half diagonally. (Or, for tea sandwiches, remove the crusts if desired and slice into 3 strips. Very dainty!)

1. Puree the olives in a food processor until smooth. Add the herbs and pulse repeatedly until all the herbs are fully incorporated. Add the sour cream, honey, salt, and pepper and blend until you have a nice, smooth spread. Taste, and adjust the seasonings as desired.

2. Cover, and store the tapenade in the refrigerator for up to a week. It can be used to make bruschetta, too!

ROASTED CUMIN CARROTS

{ MAKES 1 ½ TO 2 CUPS }

3 or 4 thick carrots

1¾ teaspoons ground cumin

2 tablespoons canola oil

½ teaspoon kosher salt

½ teaspoon freshly ground black pepper

1. Preheat the oven to 350°F.

2. Peel the carrots and cut off the tops and bottoms; then cut the carrots crosswise into thirds. Using a mandoline or a sharp knife, cut the carrots into long ⅛-inch-thick slices.

3. Place the carrot slices in a mixing bowl, and add the cumin, oil, salt, and pepper. Using clean hands, mix thoroughly, making sure all the slices are coated in oil and spices.

4. Spread the carrots evenly on a baking sheet and roast until browned (not burned), 10 to 12 minutes.

Black Forest Ham and Gruyère Sandwich

{ MAKES 1 SANDWICH }

1 tablespoon stone-ground Dijon mustard

2 slices semolina bread

1 tablespoon mayonnaise (we prefer Hellmann's)

2 thin slices Gruyère cheese

3 thin slices Black Forest ham

1 handful mesclun greens

WHO DOESN'T LOVE a great ham and cheese sammy? This one is really simple and really great. Cuts of Black Forest ham, slices of pungent Gruyère cheese, mixed greens, and stone-ground Dijon make the perfect little afternoon tea finger sandwich.

1. Spread the mustard on 1 slice of bread and the mayonnaise on the other slice.

2. Place the Gruyère and ham on 1 slice and top with the greens. Top with the other slice of bread, and slice the sandwich on the diagonal. (For tea sandwiches, slice the sandwich into 3 strips, removing the crusts if desired.)

Cucumber Watercress Sandwich with Lemon Chive Butter

{ MAKES 1 SANDWICH }

1 tablespoon Lemon Chive Butter (recipe follows)

2 slices whole-wheat bread

½ cucumber

1 handful fresh watercress

OUR TAKE ON THE traditional teatime fare adds a simple twist: Rather than offer up just a slim cucumber sandwich on buttered bread, we add lemon zest and minced chives to the butter to give it a little kick! Keep in mind that this sandwich changes dramatically depending on how you choose to cut your cucumbers; we like some crunch but prefer the cucumbers to be pretty thinly sliced. You're free to experiment with slivers, big chunks, whatever—to each his or her own!

1. Spread the lemon chive butter on both slices of bread.

2. Cut the cucumber lengthwise into ⅛-inch-thick slices. Spread the cucumber slices across 1 slice of bread, 2 or 3 slices thick. Top with the watercress and the other piece of bread. Cut the sandwich in half diagonally and serve! (For tea sandwiches, slice the sandwich into 3 strips, removing the crusts if desired.)

LEMON CHIVE BUTTER

{ MAKES 1 CUP }

2 sticks (1 cup) butter, at room temperature

Grated zest of ½ lemon

2 tablespoons minced fresh chives

Using a stand mixer, or by hand using a large spoon, cream the butter. Add the zest and chives, and mix until they are fully incorporated. Cover and refrigerate immediately to firm up. Store, covered, in the refrigerator for up to 2 weeks.

Curried Chicken Sandwich

{ MAKES 1 SANDWICH }

½ cup Curried Chicken Salad
(recipe follows)

2 slices whole-wheat bread

4 tomato slices

1 handful mixed field greens

CURRIED CHICKEN SALAD

{ MAKES 4 TO 6 SANDWICH SERVINGS }

4 medium boneless, skinless
chicken breasts

2 tablespoons curry powder

¼ cup apricot jam

¼ cup sour cream

¼ cup mayonnaise (we prefer
Hellmann's)

¼ cup finely chopped celery

¼ cup finely chopped red onion
(about ½ medium onion)

Kosher salt and freshly ground
black pepper

THIS CREAMY, CHUNKY, TANGY, zesty sandwich was a late addition but quickly topped our lists.

Place the chicken salad on 1 piece of bread, layer the tomatoes on top, and pile the mixed greens on top of that. Top it off with the other piece of bread. Cut the sandwich on the diagonal and serve! (For tea sandwiches, slice the sandwich into 3 strips, removing the crusts if desired.)

Our secret ingredient? Apricot jam for a touch of sweetness. For a great low-carb option, serve a scoop of the chicken salad over a bed of greens.

1. Preheat the oven to 350°F.

2. Rub the chicken breasts with 1 tablespoon of the curry powder, place them on a baking sheet, and roast until a meat thermometer registers 160°F in the thickest part, about 20 minutes. Let the chicken cool.

3. Meanwhile, in a large mixing bowl, combine the remaining 1 tablespoon curry powder with the apricot jam, sour cream, and mayonnaise.

4. When the chicken is cool, cut it into ½-inch cubes. Add the chicken, celery, and onion to the bowl and stir well. Season to taste with salt and pepper. (Any unused curried chicken can be covered and refrigerated for up to 5 days.)

Grilled Veggie Sandwich

{ MAKES 1 SANDWICH }

Two ¼-inch-thick eggplant slices

Four ¼-inch-thick zucchini slices

1 portobello mushroom, cut into
   ¼-inch slices

One ¼-inch-thick onion slice

¼ red pepper, cut into ¼-inch slices

Extra-virgin olive oil

Salt

2 slices pumpernickel bread

2 ounces Herbed Goat Cheese
   Spread (see page 77)

¼ cup prepared pesto spread

Two ¼-inch-thick tomato slices

THIS DELICIOUS SANDWICH is one of our most popular vegetarian options, but we have witnessed many nonveggies ordering it on a regular basis! It's healthful and hearty, with a generous amount of grilled vegetables and goat cheese.

1. Preheat the oven to 350°F. Spread the eggplant, zucchini, mushrooms, onion, and red peppers on a sheet pan and brush the vegetables with extra-virgin olive oil on both sides, then salt to taste. Roast the vegetables for about 15 minutes, or until tender.

2. Toast the bread. Spread the goat cheese spread on 1 slice and the pesto on the other. Arrange the roasted vegetables on the pesto, then add the sliced tomato. Top with the other slice of bread, cut diagonally, and serve.

Alice's BLT

{ MAKES 1 SANDWICH }

6 lean bacon strips (not too thick)

2 slices black bread

4 tablespoons Blue Cheese Spread
   (recipe follows)

1 handful mixed field greens

2 tomato slices

THE ALICE'S BLT has quickly become known as the best BLT in New York City—or so say several loyal customers, anyway. The secrets lie in the blue cheese spread, which adds some great flavor to an already flavorful sandwich, and in broiling the bacon until it is fully crisp. Yum!

1. Cook the bacon until it is crispy but not burned. (We recommend broiling the bacon on a baking sheet, about 4 minutes per side—it seals in the juices and makes it so chewy and yummy!)

2. Lightly toast the bread and place it on a cutting board. Smear one or both slices with blue cheese spread—we like it decadent, so we do both slices. Place the greens over the spread on 1 slice of bread, then top with the bacon in a crisscross pattern. Add the tomato and top with the other slice of bread. Slice on the diagonal, and serve!

BLUE CHEESE SPREAD

{ MAKES ABOUT ¼ CUP }

2 ounces blue cheese

2 tablespoons whole milk

Put the cheese in a mixer and set it on slow speed. Gradually add splashes of milk, and mix until smooth. Store, covered, in the refrigerator for up to 2 weeks.

Tuna Salad Sandwich

{ MAKES 1 SANDWICH }

½ cup *Tuna Salad (recipe follows)*

2 slices whole-wheat bread

1 handful mixed field greens

TUNA SALAD

{ MAKES 1¼ CUPS (4 TO 6
SANDWICH SERVINGS) }

*One 12-ounce can white tuna in
water, drained*

1 tablespoon capers, drained

1 tablespoon chopped cornichons

1 tablespoon minced red onion

*1 teaspoon whole-grain Dijon
mustard*

¾ teaspoon balsamic vinegar

1 teaspoon red wine vinegar

¾ teaspoon canola oil

*¾ teaspoon freshly squeezed
lemon juice*

*Kosher salt and freshly ground
black pepper*

WE DECIDED TO CREATE a tuna sandwich that was as un-deli as possible, so we threw out the mayo and brought in some punch. If you like tang in your food, you'll love it!

Put the scoop of tuna salad on 1 slice of bread and pile the mixed greens on top. Add the other slice of bread, cut the sandwich in half diagonally, and serve! (For tea sandwiches, slice the sandwich into 3 strips, removing the crusts if desired.)

1. Place the tuna in a medium mixing bowl, breaking the chunks into small pieces. Add all the remaining ingredients except the salt and pepper, and mix thoroughly. Season with salt and pepper to taste.

2. Cover and refrigerate any unused salad; it will keep for up to 5 days. It's great on a bed of greens, too!

Alice's Hummus Sandwich

{ MAKES 1 SANDWICH }

¼ cup Alice's Hummus (recipe follows)

2 slices whole-wheat bread

1 small handful mixed field greens

3 tomato slices

ALICE'S HUMMUS

{ MAKES ABOUT 2 CUPS, FOR 8 SANDWICH SERVINGS }

2 cups canned chickpeas (from one 15-ounce can), drained

3 tablespoons lemon juice (freshly squeezed, if possible)

2 tablespoons tahini (sesame paste)

2 garlic cloves, crushed

¼ cup olive oil, or more if needed

¼ teaspoon cayenne pepper

½ teaspoon ground cumin

¼ teaspoon freshly ground black pepper

¾ teaspoon sea salt

½ teaspoon paprika

THE ALICE'S HUMMUS SANDWICH was created to provide another option for our vegetarian and vegan customers.

Spread the hummus over 1 slice of bread. Place the greens on top of the hummus. Layer the tomato slices on the greens, and top with the other slice of bread. (For tea sandwiches, slice the sandwich into 3 strips, removing the crusts if desired.)

We puree our chickpeas but keep a little chunkiness, too. Fresh garlic and tahini finish it off.

Place the chickpeas in a food processor and process until finely chopped, leaving some texture/chunks. With the processor running, add all the remaining ingredients. The hummus is done when the consistency is creamy, but just a little grainy too. If it's too thick, add a bit more olive oil. Taste the hummus, and adjust the seasonings as desired.

Alice's Burgers

{ MAKES 4 BURGERS }

BURGERS

1 pound ground beef

¼ teaspoon ground allspice

2 garlic cloves, chopped

2 teaspoons Worcestershire sauce

¼ teaspoon kosher salt

*¼ teaspoon freshly ground
    black pepper*

2 teaspoons ketchup

2 teaspoons Dijon mustard

2 teaspoons whole-grain mustard

FOR COOKING

Nonstick cooking spray, if grilling

½ tablespoon butter, if sautéing

SANDWICHES

*8 slices your choice of cheese
    (optional)*

½ tablespoon butter

*1 large portobello mushroom,
    cut into strips*

¼ red onion, cut into strips

4 hamburger buns

Ketchup and mustard, as desired

LAUREN'S FRIEND LINDA wants to "marry" this burger. We know there are a lot of burgers out there claiming to be "the best," so we won't do that, but we will tell you that we doubt you'll use another recipe after trying this one . . .

1. In a medium glass or metal bowl, combine all the burger ingredients. Form the mixture into four 1-inch-thick patties.

2. *If grilling:* Spray the grill with nonstick spray before turning the heat on; then heat the grill to medium. Place the burgers on the grill and cook for about 6 minutes, or until you can slide a spatula under a burger without moving it. Flip the burgers and cook for another 6 to 8 minutes for a medium burger. (If you're using cheese, place it on the burgers immediately after flipping.)

   If using the stovetop: Melt ½ tablespoon butter in a large sauté pan over medium heat. When the pan is good and hot, place the burgers in the pan and cook for 6 minutes without disturbing (cover the pan to keep in the moisture if you like). Check to see if a spatula will slide underneath without moving the burger. If it slides easily, flip the burgers and cook for another 6 to 8 minutes for a medium burger. (If you're using cheese, place it on the burgers immediately after flipping.)

3. Before serving, slice a burger open a little to make sure the center is cooked to your liking. Cook more if needed.

4. While the burgers are cooking, place a large sauté pan over low heat and melt ½ tablespoon butter in it. When the pan is very hot, place the mushroom and onion strips on opposite sides of the pan and cook for 1 minute. Then flip the onions and mushrooms and cook for another 30 seconds.

5. To compose the burgers, place a patty on the bottom half of a bun and top with some onions and mushrooms. Add condiments and toppings, as desired, and a bun top.

Alice's Veggie Burgers

{ MAKES 4 LARGE BURGERS }

½ cup chopped cauliflower

2 rounded tablespoons Pu Erh tea leaves (see Resources)

Butter or olive oil (for sautéing)

4 medium mushrooms, finely diced

2 garlic cloves, minced

2 cups (one 15-ounce can) black-eyed peas, drained

2 egg whites

1 teaspoon sea salt or kosher salt

1 teaspoon freshly ground black pepper

3 tablespoons instant oatmeal

4 slices Gruyère cheese (optional)

4 hamburger buns

ONCE WE HAD A BURGER on our menu, there was no turning back, so we came up with a meatless option. We experimented with seemingly dozens of different ingredient combinations and finally came up with an absolutely superb veggie burger that even non-veggies adore. The star ingredients here are cauliflower and black-eyed peas, but then we take it further by infusing it with Pu Erh tea. Melt some Gruyère cheese on top and it will blow your mind . . .

1. Steam the cauliflower in a vegetable steamer set over simmering water until it is very soft and easy to mash, 4 to 6 minutes. Set aside to cool.

2. In a cup or a small bowl, steep the tea leaves in ¼ cup boiling-hot water for 3 minutes. Strain, and set the tea aside; discard the tea leaves.

Mural at Chapter III

3. Heat a little butter or oil in a sauté pan over low heat. Add the mushrooms and garlic, and cook until just soft, 5 to 7 minutes—do not brown or burn them. Set aside.

4. In a medium mixing bowl, use clean hands to combine the black-eyed peas, the steamed cauliflower, 2 teaspoons of the reserved tea, the sautéed mushrooms and garlic, and the egg whites, salt, pepper, and oatmeal. Form into 4 patties about ¾ inch thick.

5. Heat ½ teaspoon butter or oil in a large sauté pan over medium heat. Lay the patties in the pan and cook for about 6 minutes, or until a spatula will slide easily under one of the patties. Flip the patties over and cook for another 6 minutes. Flip the patties again, turn the heat to low, and cook for 5 minutes more. (If you are using the cheese, which we highly recommend, place a slice on top of each patty after you flip it and let the cheese melt in the last 5 minutes of cooking.) Remove from the heat.

6. Place the patties on hamburger buns and pile on your favorite condiments! (We suggest a handful of mixed field greens and 3 cornichons.)

NOTE: This patty is very delicate and will fall apart no matter what you do, so embrace the mess when you dive in to eat it!

Alice's Croque Monsieur

{ MAKES 1 SANDWICH }

1 tablespoon butter, at room
  temperature

2 slices raisin semolina bread

4 slices Gruyère cheese

6 thin slices Black Forest ham

WE THINK THIS IS the ultimate comfort food sandwich. We cannot count how many times over the years we've eaten one of these on a bad day, or a rainy day, or any day, really . . . Black Forest ham, Gruyère cheese, mayonnaise, and stone-ground Dijon mustard are sandwiched between two slices of raisin semolina bread and then baked until the sandwich achieves gooey, melty goodness on the inside and crispy, buttery perfection on the outside. Serve it with cornichons and be comforted . . .

1. Preheat the oven to 350°F.

2. Butter one side (which will be the outside) of each slice of bread, and lay the bread buttered side down on a baking sheet. Place 2 slices of cheese on each slice of bread, and bake until the cheese is nicely melted, about 3 minutes.

3. Place the ham on top of one of the slices of bread, and use a spatula to flip the other piece of bread onto the ham, cheese side down. Bake for 2 minutes more, or until the sandwich is nicely browned.

4. Serve with a small handful of mixed field greens and 3 cornichons or fries on the side, and enjoy!

"We were at the end of a long, tiring day in New York when the girls and I walked into Alice's Tea Cup. It was a breath of fresh air. What a perfect little restaurant for kids. And wasn't I thrilled to discover that the food is excellent, too. Imagine my shock when Sophia (age eight) asked for the Croque Monsieur. (She was right, by the way; it's an outstanding sandwich.)"

—William H. Macy

Alice's Croque Madame

{ MAKES 1 SANDWICH }

1 tablespoon butter, at room temperature

2 slices raisin semolina bread

4 slices Gruyère cheese

6 thin slices Lapsang Souchong Smoked Chicken (page 78, optional)

THIS IS HALEY'S FAVORITE SANDWICH of all time. The golden raisins and fennel in Amy's semolina bread (see Resources) add a lot of character to what's basically just a grilled cheese sandwich, and adding Lapsang Souchong Smoked Chicken makes it even better! Buttered on the outside for the perfect crispy exterior, this sandwich is a sure crowd-pleaser.

1. Preheat the oven to 350°F.

2. Butter one side (which will be the outside) of each slice of bread, and lay the bread buttered side down on a baking sheet. Place 2 slices of cheese on each slice of bread, and bake until the cheese is nicely melted, about 3 minutes. (If you're using the chicken, place it on top of one of the slices before the cheese.)

3. Use a spatula to flip the other piece of bread on top, cheese side down. Bake for 2 minutes more, or until the sandwich is nicely browned.

4. Serve with a small handful of mixed field greens and 3 cornichons or fries on the side, and enjoy!

Alice's King Reuben

{ MAKES 1 SANDWICH }

1 tablespoon butter, at room
   temperature

2 slices raisin semolina bread

4 slices Gruyère cheese

6 thin slices Lapsang Souchong
   Smoked Chicken (page 78)

¼ cup sauerkraut, drained

2 tablespoons Thousand Island
   dressing

WE TOOK THE CROQUE MADAME, added our tea-smoked chicken, some sauerkraut, and Thousand Island dressing, and *voilà*—our own reuben! It's a favorite of ours, and of tons of customers.

1. Preheat the oven to 350°F.

2. Butter one side (which will be the outside) of each slice of bread, and lay the bread buttered side down on a baking sheet. Place 2 slices of cheese on each slice of bread, and bake until the cheese is nicely melted, about 3 minutes.

3. Layer the chicken, sauerkraut, and dressing onto one of the pieces of bread. Then use a spatula to flip the other piece of bread onto it, cheese side down. Bake for 2 minutes more, or until the sandwich is nicely browned.

4. Serve with a small handful of mixed field greens and 3 cornichons or fries on the side, and enjoy!

Nutella and Granny Smith Apple Sandwich

{ MAKES 1 SANDWICH }

2 slices white bread

2 tablespoons Nutella

½ Granny Smith apple, cored (but not peeled) and cut into ⅛-inch-thick slices

WOW, THIS SANDWICH is popular . . . and it is *so simple*! We wanted to give kids a sandwich with a chocolate element, but nothing *too* chocolatey. Nutella is a favorite with everyone because it's sweet enough to pass kids' taste tests but not so sweet or "dessert" that it turns off parents. Adding Granny Smith apples cuts some of that sweetness and adds some tang (not to mention something healthier to the mix).

Spread each slice of bread with 1 tablespoon Nutella. Lay the apple slices across one slice of bread, then top with the other slice. Slice in half diagonally.

Homemade Peanut Butter on Granny Smith Apple Slices

MAKES 1 SERVING

Green apples for tangy sweetness served with our homemade peanut butter make a great and *quick* snack that is both healthy and packed with protein for good, high energy. (Warning: Adults enjoy this, too!)

3 tablespoons homemade peanut butter (recipe follows)

Granny Smith apple, cored (but not peeled) and cut into ⅛-inch-thick slices

Scoop the peanut butter into a small bowl or ramekin, and place it in the center of a plate. Fan the apple slices around the bowl. Time to dip!

PB&J on Banana Bread

{ MAKES 1 SANDWICH }

2 slices Sue's Magical Banana Bread (page 161)

2 tablespoons Homemade Peanut Butter (recipe follows)

2 tablespoons raspberry jam

HOMEMADE PEANUT BUTTER

{ MAKES ABOUT 2 CUPS }

2½ cups plain unsalted peanuts

½ teaspoon kosher salt

1 tablespoon honey

2 tablespoons peanut oil

OUR AMAZING BAKER SUE makes the best banana bread, hands down! So of course we needed to use it for a kids' sandwich. Healthy, fresh, moist, and flavorful, the banana bread *makes* this meal, while the usual white bread would just be a vehicle for the PB&J.

Spread 1 slice of bread with the peanut butter and the other with the jam. Put the two slices together and cut in half.

We started making our own peanut butter so that we could control the creaminess—it's sort of a combination of chunky and creamy.

Combine the peanuts, salt, and honey in a food processor, and process for about 1 minute. Scrape down the bowl, cover, and process for 1 to 2 minutes while slowly drizzling in the oil. Leave some small chunks in the peanut butter. Cover and store in the refrigerator. Stir to recombine before serving.

Ellen, with a PB&J on Banana Bread

Cookies

✦ ✦ ✦

Whenever you're baking cookies, keep a camera nearby. Sure, if you have kids, there's nothing cuter than photos of them stealing dough or getting chocolate on their faces, but it's fun for adults, too—we've been known to snap camera-phone pics of our baking for all our friends to admire on Facebook! Cookies are easy to bake but quite impressive to the happy recipients of your efforts. What could be more satisfying?

We make a lot of different cookies at Alice's, but we chose the particular recipes in this book because either they're great to serve at parties or they're simply the best of their kind and we had to share! Oh, and to stay with the theme of so many of our recipes, we add tea to our cookies whenever possible!

Ginger-Molasses Cookies

2¼ cups all-purpose flour

2 teaspoons baking soda

¼ teaspoon kosher salt

1 teaspoon ground cinnamon

1 teaspoon ground ginger

½ teaspoon ground cloves

1½ sticks (¾ cup) unsalted
  butter, at room temperature

1 cup firmly packed dark
  brown sugar

¼ cup granulated sugar

1 egg

¼ cup molasses

SUE, OUR "MASTER BAKER," worked really hard to get this recipe just right without resorting to shortening to make the cookies chewy. The result is a chewy, spicy ginger cookie just like Mom made 'em. . . .

1. Preheat the oven to 350°F.

2. In a medium bowl, combine the flour, baking soda, salt, and spices. Set aside.

3. Use a mixer to cream the butter and sugars in a large bowl. Add the egg and molasses, and mix until smooth and well blended. With the mixer at its lowest setting, mix in the dry ingredients a little bit at a time, until the mixture is well incorporated and you have a workable dough.

4. Using an ice cream scoop, scoop the dough onto a nonstick cookie sheet, spacing the scoops 2 inches apart. Use the back of the ice cream scoop to press the top of each cookie down slightly, so there is a 2-inch flat surface on each.

5. Bake for 12 to 15 minutes, or until lightly browned. Let cool for 15 to 20 minutes.

Peanut Butter Chocolate Chip Cookies

{ MAKES 20 TO 24 COOKIES }

3 cups all-purpose flour

1 teaspoon baking soda

1 teaspoon kosher salt

2 sticks (1 cup) unsalted butter, at room temperature

1 cup granulated sugar

1 cup firmly packed dark brown sugar

2 eggs

1 teaspoon pure vanilla extract

2 cups creamy peanut butter

2 cups mini chocolate chips

OUR ENTIRE FAMILY has a peanut butter obsession—especially Haley's husband, Michael. We also think that nothing goes better with peanut butter than chocolate, so we sought to make a peanut butter–filled chocolate chip cookie that was thick and rich. We think we really succeeded with this one . . .

1. Preheat the oven to 350°F.

2. In a medium bowl, combine the flour, baking soda, and salt. Set aside.

3. Use a mixer to cream the butter and sugars in a large mixing bowl. Add the eggs, mixing them in one at a time, and the vanilla, and mix until smooth. Add in the dry mixture a bit at a time, mixing as you go until it is fully incorporated. Add the peanut butter and mix until the batter is creamy. Using a silicone spatula, fold in the chocolate chips.

4. Using an ice cream scoop, scoop the dough onto a nonstick baking sheet, spacing the scoops 3 inches apart. Use the back of the scoop to pat down the tops of the cookies so that there is about a 2-inch flat surface on each one. Press each cookie with the back of a fork to make a crisscross pattern.

5. Bake for 12 to 14 minutes, or until lightly browned. Let cool on the baking sheet for 15 to 20 minutes.

Rooibos Phoenix Oatmeal Butterscotch Chip Cookies

{ MAKES 20 TO 24 COOKIES }

4 heaping teaspoons
    Rooibos Phoenix tea leaves
    (see Resources)

3 sticks (1½ cups) unsalted butter,
    at room temperature

2½ cups turbinado sugar

4 eggs

3 cups all-purpose flour

2 teaspoons baking soda

1½ teaspoons ground cinnamon

1 teaspoon kosher salt

6 cups 2-minute quick-cooking Irish
    oatmeal (such as McCann's)

3 cups Hershey's butterscotch chips

THIS IS A SOFT oatmeal cookie that is infused with Rooibos Phoenix tea (a caramel, honey, and vanilla flavored tea) and filled with tons of butterscotch chips. Lauren has a love/hate relationship with these: she loves them, and she hates that she can't resist them! Be careful—it could happen to you, too.

1. Steep the tea leaves in ¼ cup boiling-hot water for 7 minutes. Strain the tea, discarding the tea leaves, and refrigerate the tea for 15 minutes to cool it down.

2. Meanwhile, preheat the oven to 375°F.

3. Use a mixer to cream the butter and sugar in a large bowl. Add the cooled tea and the eggs, and beat until smooth.

4. In a separate bowl, mix together the flour, baking soda, cinnamon, and salt.

5. With the mixer running, add the dry ingredients to the butter-sugar mixture, a little bit at a time, until everything is well incorporated. Use a spatula to hand-mix the oatmeal and butterscotch chips into the dough.

6. Drop heaping tablespoons of the dough onto a nonstick baking sheet, spacing them about 2 inches apart (they will spread quite a bit).

7. Bake for 15 to 18 minutes, until the tops of the cookies are slightly browned. Let cool on the baking sheet and *devour* these yummies!

Queen of Hearts Linzer Card Cookies

{ MAKES 20 TO 24 COOKIES }

4 sticks (2 cups) unsalted butter,
    at room temperature

2 cups granulated sugar

2 eggs

1 tablespoon pure vanilla extract

6 cups all-purpose flour, plus extra
    for rolling

1 tablespoon baking powder

1 teaspoon kosher salt

1 to 1½ cups seedless raspberry jam

Confectioners' sugar, for sprinkling

ADMITTEDLY, IT'S HOW these cookies look that sells them, but they're the real thing—masterful buttery cookies and perfectly complementary raspberry preserves. Of course we had to make Alice's "house of cards" in a cookie, just to add a hint of Wonderland playfulness to the cookie tray!

1. Use a mixer to cream the butter and granulated sugar in a large bowl. Add the eggs, mixing them in one at a time, and then the vanilla, and mix until well incorporated. Combine the flour, baking powder, and salt in a medium bowl. With the mixer on its lowest speed, slowly add the dry mixture. Mix until you have a workable dough. Cover the dough and refrigerate it for at least 1 hour, until firm.

2. When you're ready to bake the cookies, preheat the oven to 400°F.

3. On a lightly floured surface, roll out the dough to a ¼-inch thickness. Using a rectangular cookie cutter about the size of a playing card (2 × 3 inches), cut out the cookies, placing them 1 inch apart on several nonstick baking sheets as you go. Gather the remaining dough, roll it out, and cut out more cookies.

4. Using a small heart-shaped cookie cutter (about 1½ inches in diameter), cut out the centers of half of the cookies. (You can set the heart shapes aside and bake them separately; they're wonderful with red and pink royal icing—see sidebar, page 110.)

5. Bake the cookies for 6 to 8 minutes, or until ever so slightly browned. Set aside to cool completely on the baking sheets.

(continued)

Yossy making the Queen of Hearts Linzer Card Cookies

6. Take one of the plain (non-heart-cut) cookies, and using a small offset spatula, spread a ⅛-inch-thick layer of jam neatly and evenly over it, covering the top of the cookie completely. Repeat with all the plain cookies.

7. Lay the heart-cut cookies on a clean surface and sprinkle them with confectioners' sugar. Holding the sides of the heart-cut cookies, carefully place one on top of each jam-covered cookie, lining them up perfectly. Yay! That was pretty easy, no?

Iced Hearts

If you bake the little hearts separately, let them cool completely, and then use an offset spatula to spread colored royal icing on them. Be careful not to cover them or disturb the tops for at least 12 hours, because it takes at least that long for the icing to fully harden.

Royal Icing

1 pound confectioners' sugar

¼ cup meringue powder

Sift the powdered sugar and meringue powder together into a mixing bowl. With a mixer running at its lowest speed, slowly drizzle in ½ cup water, mixing constantly until the icing is completely smooth. Cover with plastic to keep the air out, as it dries quickly!

You can divide the icing and add the colors of your choice to smaller portions. We like to use gel colors, which you can order online or find at bakers' specialty stores. You need very little gel to color the icing—just dip a toothpick in the color, put it in the icing, and mix the icing to distribute the color, adding more color as needed. Be sure to wrap the icing in plastic if you're not working with it, because it starts to harden quickly.

There are so many different ways to use this icing to decorate, from spreading it to piping it in patterns or layers. Let your imagination run wild and have fun!

Rooibos Africana Ranger Cookies

{ MAKES 20 TO 24 COOKIES }

2 teaspoons Rooibos Africana tea leaves (see Resources)

2½ cups all-purpose flour

1 teaspoon baking powder

1 teaspoon baking soda

2 sticks (1 cup) unsalted butter, at room temperature

1 cup granulated sugar

1 cup firmly packed dark brown sugar

2 eggs

2 teaspoons pure vanilla extract

4 cups Rice Krispies

2½ cups sweetened shredded coconut

½ cup raisins

WE LOVE THIS CRUNCHY cookie so much, with its Rice Krispies, shredded coconut, and raisins intermingling with a Rooibos Africana tea infusion (one of our favorite teas). These cookies give you chewy and crunchy at the same time, along with a truly unique flavor!

1. Preheat the oven to 350°F.

2. In a coffee or spice grinder, grind the tea leaves to a fine powder.

3. Combine the flour, baking powder, baking soda, and powdered tea in a medium bowl, and set aside.

4. In a large bowl, use a mixer to cream the butter and sugars. With the mixer on low, add the eggs one at a time, then the vanilla. Mix until fully combined and smooth. Slowly mix in the dry mixture until all is fully incorporated. Using a spatula, hand-mix the Rice Krispies, coconut flakes, and raisins into the dough.

5. Using an ice cream scoop, scoop the dough onto a nonstick baking sheet, spacing the scoops 3 inches apart. Use the back of the scoop to pat down the tops of the cookies slightly, until there is about a 2-inch flat surface on each.

6. Bake for 12 to 14 minutes, or until lightly browned. Cool on the baking sheet for 15 to 20 minutes.

Thumbprint Cookies

{ MAKES 20 TO 24 COOKIES }

2 sticks (1 cup) unsalted butter,
  at room temperature

½ cup sugar

Grated zest of ½ orange

1½ teaspoons pure vanilla extract

3 egg yolks

2¼ cups all-purpose flour

¾ teaspoon kosher salt

⅓ cup jam (your favorite flavor)

WE WANTED TO OFFER both a shortbread cookie and a linzer cookie. Done and done in one!

1. Preheat the oven to 375°F.

2. Using a mixer, cream the butter and sugar in a large bowl until smooth. One ingredient at a time, add the orange zest, vanilla, and egg yolks and mix until smooth. With the mixer on its lowest setting, add the flour and salt and mix until all the ingredients are fully incorporated. You should now have a firm, workable dough.

3. Using a melon baller, scoop the dough onto a nonstick baking sheet, spacing the scoops about 1½ inches apart. Use your thumb to press down in the center of each dough ball, creating a small pocket for the jam. Fill each thumbprint with a small dollop of jam.

4. Bake for 10 to 15 minutes, or until just so slightly browned. Be sure to let the cookies cool thoroughly on the baking sheet before eating—the jam will be hot!

Hello Dolly Bars (page 163) and Thumbprint Cookies

Double Chocolate Cookies

{ MAKES 10 TO 12
LARGE COOKIES }

2 teaspoons Mauritius tea leaves
(see Resources)

3 cups all-purpose flour

1 cup unsweetened cocoa powder
(we recommend Hershey's)

1 teaspoon baking soda

1 teaspoon kosher salt

1 cup dark chocolate pistoles or
good-quality semisweet chocolate
chunks (see Note)

2 sticks (1 cup) unsalted butter,
at room temperature

3 cups granulated sugar

4 eggs

2 teaspoons pure vanilla extract

1 cup semisweet chocolate chips

½ cup coarse turbinado sugar

OH, YOUR FRIENDS WILL be torn between love and hate when you bring these to a party—but make them anyway! They're so rich and chocolatey that it is almost impossible to stop eating them. The rock sugar sprinkled on top adds the perfect amount of sweetness to what is not an overly sweet cookie.

1. Preheat the oven to 350°F.

2. In a coffee or spice grinder, grind the tea leaves to a fine powder. Set aside.

3. Combine the flour, cocoa powder, baking soda, salt, and powdered tea in a medium bowl and set aside.

4. Melt the chocolate pistoles in a double boiler, in a microwave oven, or in a Pyrex bowl over a hot water bath. Be very careful not to burn the chocolate!

5. Use a mixer to cream the butter and granulated sugar in a large bowl. With the mixer on low, add the melted chocolate, eggs (one at a time), and vanilla extract, and then the dry ingredients. Mix until fully incorporated and smooth. Use a spatula to fold the chocolate chips in by hand.

6. Using a small ice cream scoop, scoop out the dough onto a nonstick baking sheet, spacing the scoops about 2 inches apart. Use the back of the scoop to pat down the tops of the cookies so that there is a flat surface on each one. Sprinkle about 1 teaspoon of turbinado sugar on the top of each cookie.

7. Bake for 12 to 15 minutes, until the tops appear slightly crispy. Let cool on the baking sheet for 15 to 20 minutes.

NOTE: We recommend Cacao Barry Dark "Favorites Mi-Amère" Pistoles if you can get them. If not, Baker's Semi-Sweet Chocolate will also work.

The Red Queen's Pink and White Chessboard Cookies

{ MAKES 100 TO 125 COOKIES }

4 heaping teaspoons Rose
    Tea Mélange tea leaves
    (see Resources)

4 cups all-purpose flour, plus
    extra for dusting

1 teaspoon baking powder

2½ sticks (1¼ cups) unsalted
    butter, at room temperature

1 cup sugar

2 whole eggs

Red food coloring

1 egg white

OUR SHORTBREAD MELTS ON the tongue—the rich taste of the butter is amazing! Make these using any colors you wish; this heavenly version is infused with our Rose Tea Mélange. People always bite off a darker square first. Test it out yourself—it's funny! These take quite a bit of time to make, but they're actually pretty easy, so put on some music and devote an afternoon to it!

1. Steep the tea leaves in ½ cup boiling-hot water for 2 minutes. Then strain the tea and discard the tea leaves. Cover the tea and place it in the freezer to cool quickly.

2. Combine the flour and baking powder in a medium bowl and set it aside.

3. In a large bowl, use a mixer to cream the butter and sugar until smooth. Add the 2 whole eggs and 3 teaspoons of the cooled tea (reserve the remaining tea), and mix until all the ingredients are thoroughly combined and smooth. With the mixer set on the lowest speed, slowly add in the dry ingredients until you have a workable dough.

4. Divide the dough in half and put one half back in the mixer. With the mixer set on the lowest speed, add 2 to 4 drops red food coloring to the dough, and mix until the dough is a consistent pink color.

5. Roll each portion of dough into a 1-inch-thick square. Wrap the squares in plastic wrap, and refrigerate for at least 1 hour, until firm, to set the dough.

6. Flour two baking sheets. On a floured surface, roll each piece of dough into a ⅜-inch-thick rectangle. Lay the rectangles on the baking sheets, cover them with plastic wrap, and refrigerate until set, about 2 hours.

7. Make an egg wash by lightly beating the egg white with 2 teaspoons of the reserved tea. Do not let it thicken or form peaks!

8. To create the fancy cookie pattern, you start by making alternating white and pink layers of dough: Remove the plastic wrap from the white dough, and brush the top with some of the egg wash. (You will use more of this mixture; cover and refrigerate it until you need it again.) Remove the plastic wrap from the pink dough, and carefully place the pink dough on top of the white dough. Use the empty cookie sheet to press lightly on the top of the two doughs so that they stick to each other—but don't smush them too much!

9. Cut the dough in half crosswise, to make two squares of double-layer dough. Brush one of the squares with egg wash and repeat the last step, layering the other square on top and pressing the dough stack lightly with the cookie sheet. Gently wrap the dough in plastic wrap and refrigerate it for at least 1 hour—more if possible—to get it to set firmly.

10. Unwrap the dough again and place it on a cutting board. Use a very sharp nonserrated knife to cut the dough lengthwise into sixteen $3/8$-inch-wide strips.

11. Now it's time to make the checkerboard pattern! Lightly flour a work surface and lay out 1 strip of dough with the cut side down. Brush the top with egg wash. Take another dough strip and lay it on top, making sure the color order is reversed—pink on top of white and white on top of pink. Repeat with 2 more dough strips, brushing with egg wash to help seal the surface.

(continued)

12. Repeat with the remaining dough strips so that you end up with 4 long dough blocks, each with 4 layers of dough. Gently press the sides of each dough block so that you have a good squared-off surface on all four sides. Carefully wrap each dough block in plastic wrap and refrigerate for at least 1 hour.

13. Preheat the oven to 350°F.

14. Unwrap the dough blocks and lay them on a cutting board. Using a very sharp, clean nonserrated knife, make the cookies by cutting each dough block into ¼-inch-thick slices. To make sure the dough keeps its shape, turn the block over after each slice, clean the knife as needed, and cut very slowly, being careful not to mash the dough at all. As you cut out each cookie, lay it on a nonstick baking sheet, at least 1 inch away from the other cookies. If you fill more baking sheets than you can bake at one time, cover the baking sheets in plastic wrap and refrigerate them until ready.

15. Bake the cookies for 12 to 15 minutes, but don't let them brown! Set them aside to cool on the baking sheet. Yay, you did it! It was a lot of work, but your friends will be *so* impressed! And the cookies taste as good as they look, with a subtle rose flavor. Enjoy!

The Red Queen's Pink and White Chessboard Cookies
and Queen of Hearts Linzer Card Cookies (page 109)

Cakes and Cupcakes

✦ ✦ ✦

Whether it's for a party, or as a little something for your significant other, or simply because you just want to eat cake today, a good cake brings its own celebration. And there are lots of easy ways to get a little fancy with colored sugars, cutout shapes, and piped icing. Making cakes and cupcakes is great fun, and there's nothing better to have on hand, whether for guests or for your 4:00 a.m. cravings!

As much as we love our pumpkin scones—and we love them intensely—worth at least as much praise is our mother's signature cake, which we call "Jean's Not-Yet-but-Soon-to-Be-Famous Mocha Chocolate Chip Cake" (page 123). We were raised on this cake, and although we don't remember the espresso keeping us up all night, we're sure it contributed energy to some late-night Scrabble sessions!

> **✦ Tip ✦**
> The single greatest baking tool is the offset spatula. Meet your new best baking friend!

The cakes and cupcakes here have a place in Alice's hall of fame for different reasons—some are simply too good to be vegan, some are too moist to be cake—but the thing we strive for in cakes and cupcakes is the perfect balance. A cake must be the right combination of salty and sweet, buttery but not too buttery, cakey but not dry . . . If these elements are in place, that's a cake for the hall of fame.

Fin eating chocolate cake

Jean's Not-Yet-but-Soon-to-Be-Famous Mocha Chocolate Chip Cake

{ MAKES ONE 8-INCH
2-LAYER CAKE }

CAKE

*1 stick (½ cup) salted butter,
at room temperature*

1½ cups turbinado sugar

2 eggs

1½ teaspoons pure vanilla extract

*2¼ cups sifted all-purpose flour
(we prefer Hecker's unbleached
flour)*

2½ teaspoons baking powder

1 level teaspoon kosher salt

*1 cup plus 2 tablespoons 2% or
whole milk*

*¾ to 1 cup semisweet chocolate
chips, to taste*

THANKS, MOM! Life just wouldn't have been the same without this cake. We've had it as our birthday cake and holiday cake for our entire lives, but it has also taken on a life of its own—several friends have even requested it as their wedding cake, and Mom has been happy to oblige. If you like coffee (coffee to drink, coffee ice cream, iced mocha lattes, or all of the above), prepare to never make another cake again! Our mother says, "You're welcome."

1. *To make the cake*, preheat the oven to 350°F, and butter and flour two 8-inch round cake pans. Set them aside.

2. In a large mixing bowl, cream the butter and sugar by hand. Add the eggs and vanilla, and mix well.

3. In a medium bowl, combine the flour, baking powder, and salt, also by hand. Add half of the flour mixture to the wet mixture, and mix thoroughly. Then mix in half of the milk, followed by the remaining flour mixture, and then the remaining milk, mixing after each addition. Add the chocolate chips, and mix again.

4. Pour the batter into the prepared cake pans and bake for 30 to 35 minutes, or until the cake has pulled away from the sides of the pan and a toothpick inserted into the center comes out clean. Set the cake layers aside on a wire rack to cool thoroughly before removing from the pans and frosting.

(continued)

FROSTING

4 heaping teaspoons Medaglia D'Oro instant espresso powder

3½ cups (one 1-pound box) confectioners' sugar

1 stick (½ cup) salted butter, at room temperature

⅛ teaspoon kosher salt

½ teaspoon pure vanilla extract

¾ to 1 cup semisweet chocolate chips

5. *To make the frosting,* combine the espresso powder with 3 to 5 teaspoons boiling-hot water (use less water for a strong mocha flavor and more water for a milder flavor). Set aside.

6. In a large mixing bowl, thoroughly mix one-third of the confectioners' sugar with the butter, salt, and vanilla. Add the next one-third of the sugar, then the final third, mixing well after each addition. Add the espresso a little at a time, mixing well as you go, until the frosting has reached the desired consistency. Add the chocolate chips and mix again.

7. *To build the cake,* frost both layers and stack them; then frost the sides of the cake. (Be sure to wait until the layers have cooled fully; you don't want to melt the chocolate chips!)

"I wonder if it's possible to survive on nothing but cakes and scones; if it is, they could only be from Alice's."

—Raul Esparza

Mom making her mocha cake

Chocolate Cake with Vanilla Buttercream

{ MAKES ONE 8-INCH
3-LAYER CAKE }

2 cups sugar

1¾ cups all-purpose flour

¾ cup unsweetened cocoa powder
  (we recommend Hershey's)

1½ teaspoons baking soda

1½ teaspoons baking powder

1 teaspoon kosher salt

¼ cup sour cream

2 eggs

1 cup whole milk

½ cup canola oil

1 teaspoon pure vanilla extract

¾ cup hot brewed coffee

The Yummiest Vanilla Buttercream
  Frosting (recipe follows)

THIS IS THE BEST chocolate cake ever—no contest. It's thoroughly moist (thanks to the coffee in the batter), with not too rich a chocolate and not too buttery a frosting. It has been praised online by our new friends Blondie and Brownie of Just Desserts NYC: "The buttercream is thick and sweet, generously spread between each layer. The cake is so moist, it tastes like an Oreo cookie dunked in milk. It is *the best* cake in NYC." Lauren says most cakes are just a conduit for the frosting, but not ours . . . See for yourself!

1. *To make the cake,* preheat the oven to 350°F, and have ready three 8-inch round nonstick cake pans.

2. In a large bowl, sift together the sugar, flour, cocoa powder, baking soda, baking powder, and salt.

3. With a mixer on medium speed, add the sour cream, eggs (one at a time), milk, oil, and vanilla to the dry ingredients, and keep mixing for exactly 2 minutes. Scrape down the bowl. With the mixer on low speed, slowly drizzle in the hot coffee, mixing until the batter is blended and smooth. It will be very liquidy—this is good!

4. Divide the batter evenly among the cake pans, and bake for 20 to 25 minutes, or until a toothpick inserted into the center of the cakes comes out clean. Set the layers aside on a wire rack to cool completely before removing from the pans and frosting.

5. *To build the cake,* frost all three layers with the buttercream and then stack the layers; then frost the sides of the cake.

NOTE: We're partial to The Yummiest Vanilla Buttercream Frosting for this cake, but you can use any frosting your heart desires!

THE YUMMIEST VANILLA BUTTERCREAM FROSTING

2 sticks (1 cup) unsalted butter, at room temperature

1 pound confectioners' sugar

2 tablespoons whole milk, at room temperature

½ teaspoon pure vanilla extract

With a mixer on medium speed, cream the butter in a large mixing bowl. Reduce the speed to low and add the confectioners' sugar a little bit at a time, alternating with splashes of the milk and the vanilla. Mix until the frosting is smooth.

Betina painting a sugar butterfly

Peanut Butter Ganache Cake

{ MAKES ONE 8-INCH
3-LAYER CAKE }

*1 recipe Chocolate Cake
(page 126; cake recipe only)*

PEANUT BUTTER FROSTING

*2 sticks (1 cup) unsalted butter,
at room temperature*

*1¼ cups cream cheese, at room
temperature*

1 cup creamy peanut butter

5 cups confectioners' sugar

*1 tablespoon milk, or more if
needed, at room temperature*

CHOCOLATE–PEANUT
BUTTER GANACHE

*4 ounces bittersweet chocolate
(such as Baker's chocolate)*

*1½ tablespoons creamy peanut
butter*

1 tablespoon Karo light corn syrup

¼ cup heavy cream

THIS CAKE IS SO BRILLIANT, it makes us smile just thinking of it. The amount of peanut butter in it makes it moist and almost chewy—you'll just have to see for yourself!

1. First, bake the cake layers as described on page 126. While the layers are cooling, prepare the peanut butter frosting and the chocolate–peanut butter ganache.

2. *To make the peanut butter frosting,* use a mixer to cream the butter, cream cheese, and peanut butter in a large bowl until smooth. On the lowest speed, slowly add the confectioners' sugar, adding the milk when the frosting gets too thick. Mix until all is fully incorporated and smooth. Add a little more milk if necessary, but be very careful not to make the frosting too loose.

3. *To make the chocolate–peanut butter ganache,* combine all the ganache ingredients in a small saucepan over the lowest heat, stirring constantly until all is fully incorporated and smooth. Do not bring to a simmer. Let cool just a bit before pouring onto the cake.

4. *To build the cake,* frost all three layers with the peanut butter frosting and stack the layers. Frost the sides of the cake as well. Pour the ganache over the center of the top of the cake, so that it spreads out evenly across the top and drizzles down the sides. Serve immediately for maximum oohs and aahs!

Banana Nutella Cake

{ MAKES ONE 8-INCH 3-LAYER CAKE }

CAKE

3 cups all-purpose flour

1½ teaspoons baking soda

¾ teaspoon kosher salt

1½ sticks (¾ cup) unsalted butter, at room temperature

2 cups sugar

3 eggs

1½ cups buttermilk

1 teaspoon pure vanilla extract

2 very ripe bananas, mashed

CREAM CHEESE FROSTING

1 stick (½ cup) butter, at room temperature

1½ cups cream cheese, at room temperature

3 cups confectioners' sugar

FILLING AND DECORATION

2 cups Nutella (you'll need two 13-ounce jars)

ONE OF OUR BRILLIANT bakers thought to incorporate our highly popular banana bread with Nutella and our cream cheese frosting. We even pipe Nutella on top of the cake!

1. *To make the cake,* preheat the oven to 350°F, and have ready three 8-inch round nonstick cake pans.

2. In a medium bowl, whisk the dry ingredients together.

3. In a large bowl, use a mixer to cream the butter and sugar until light and fluffy. One at a time, add the eggs and mix until well blended. With the mixer set to low, add a little bit of the flour mixture at a time, alternating with the buttermilk and vanilla, mixing just until smooth. Use a spatula to gently fold in the mashed bananas.

4. Pour the batter evenly into the three cake pans, and bake for 20 to 25 minutes, or until a toothpick inserted into the center of the cakes comes out clean. Set the layers aside to cool completely in the pans before frosting the cake.

5. *To make the frosting,* use a mixer to cream the butter and cream cheese in a large bowl until fully combined and smooth. With the mixer set on the lowest speed, slowly add the confectioners' sugar, mixing until it is completely incorporated and the frosting is smooth.

6. Frost each layer with Nutella (you won't use it all) and stack them. Spread the cream cheese frosting over the top and sides. Using a piping bag with a 12- or 14-mm tip, pipe five concentric circles of Nutella around the top of the cake, starting with a small one in the center and increasing the size of the circles as you work your way out. Run a butter knife from the center outward, across the top of the frosting, alternating with scores in the opposite direction (outer circle to the center) until you have gone around the cake.

Carrot Cake

4 eggs

1½ cups canola oil

2 cups sugar

2 cups all-purpose flour

2 teaspoons baking soda

2 teaspoons ground cinnamon

1 teaspoon kosher salt

3 cups grated carrots

1 cup raisins

1 cup chopped walnuts

3 cups Cream Cheese Frosting
(page 133)

LIKE WHITE CAKES, carrot cakes are known for drying out too quickly—but not this one! The generous use of carrots and raisins adds freshness and natural sweetness to the batter.

1. *To make the cake,* preheat the oven to 350°F, and have ready three 8-inch round nonstick cake pans.

2. In a large bowl, whisk the eggs, oil, and sugar together until smooth. Combine the flour, baking soda, cinnamon, and salt in a medium bowl. Fold the flour mixture into the wet mix, just until incorporated. Gently fold in the carrots, raisins, and walnuts.

3. Pour the batter evenly into the three cake pans, and bake for 20 to 25 minutes, or until the top is slightly browned. Let cool thoroughly in the pans before frosting.

4. *To build the cake,* frost all three layers with cream cheese frosting and stack the layers; then frost the sides of the cake.

Coconut Cake

{ MAKES ONE 8-INCH }
{ 3-LAYER CAKE }

CAKE

3 teaspoons Rooibos Coconut
  Vanilla tea leaves (see
  Resources)

2¼ cups all-purpose flour

2½ teaspoons baking powder

¼ teaspoon kosher salt

2 sticks (1 cup) unsalted butter,
  at room temperature

1½ cups sugar

3 large eggs

½ teaspoon pure vanilla extract

¾ cup heavy cream

COCONUT FILLING

2 teaspoons Rooibos
  Coconut Vanilla tea leaves
  (see Resources)

1¼ cups heavy cream

¾ cup sugar

1 stick (½ cup) unsalted butter

1½ tablespoons cornstarch

2¼ cups sweetened shredded
  coconut

THIS PRETTY CAKE IS easy to make and great for parties! Frost it with vanilla buttercream or cream cheese frosting—both are amazing. The secret weapon here is the coconut "custard" filling between the layers. And you can never use too much coconut on the outside of the cake—basically as much as you can stick on it. A fun activity for kids or adults!

1. *To make the cake,* preheat the oven to 350°F, and have ready three 8-inch round nonstick cake pans.

2. Steep the tea leaves in ¼ cup boiling-hot water for 10 minutes. Strain, discarding the tea leaves, and set the tea aside to cool.

3. In a medium bowl, sift the flour, baking powder, and salt together.

4. In a large bowl, use a mixer to cream the butter and sugar until very light. With the mixer on medium speed, add the eggs, one at a time, and then the vanilla extract, mixing after each addition. With the mixer at its lowest setting, alternate adding the flour mixture, cream, and the cooled tea, mixing until the batter is smooth.

5. Pour the batter evenly into the three cake pans, and bake for 20 to 25 minutes, or until lightly browned. Set aside to cool thoroughly in the pans before filling and frosting.

6. *To make the coconut filling,* steep the tea leaves in 2 tablespoons boiling-hot water for 10 minutes. Strain, and set the tea aside to cool.

(continued)

2 cups *The Yummiest Vanilla Buttercream Frosting (page 129) or Cream Cheese Frosting (page 133)*

Sweetened shredded coconut, for coating

7. Bring the cream, sugar, and butter to a boil in a medium saucepan over medium heat, stirring occasionally until all the sugar has dissolved.

8. In a small bowl, mix the cornstarch and 1 tablespoon of the cooled Rooibos tea. Add this to the cream mixture and bring to a boil, stirring until thickened.

9. Pulse the coconut in a food processor until very finely chopped, and place it in a large bowl. Remove the cream mixture from the heat and strain it over the chopped coconut. Cover the filling and refrigerate for at least 1 hour. Just before using, whip the mixture in a stand mixer fitted with the paddle attachment until smooth and creamy.

10. *To build the cake,* spread the coconut filling over two of the layers, and stack the layers. Frost the top and sides of the cake with the vanilla buttercream or cream cheese frosting. Then coat the whole cake with as much coconut as your heart desires!

Blueberry Lemon Cake

{ MAKES ONE 8-INCH
3-LAYER CAKE }

3⅓ cups all-purpose flour

½ teaspoon kosher salt

½ teaspoon baking powder

½ teaspoon baking soda

1½ sticks (¾ cup) unsalted butter,
    at room temperature

2 cups sugar

⅓ cup freshly squeezed lemon juice

1 teaspoon freshly grated
    lemon zest

4 eggs

1 cup plus 2 tablespoons buttermilk

2½ cups blueberries

The Yummiest Vanilla Buttercream
    Frosting (page 129)

OUR FATHER IS THE official sweet tooth in the family, and he's a sucker for all things lemon-flavored. You should have seen his eyes widen when we first presented this moist, tangy, lemon zest–filled cake packed with fresh blueberries—and, of course, topped with our buttercream frosting.

1. *To make the cake,* preheat the oven to 350°F, and lightly butter and flour three 8-inch round nonstick cake pans.

2. In a medium mixing bowl, sift the flour, salt, baking powder, and baking soda together.

3. In a large bowl, use a mixer to cream the butter and sugar. Then add the lemon juice and zest, and mix until smooth. Add the eggs, mixing them in one at a time, and mix until fully combined. With the mixer set to the lowest speed, alternate adding the dry mixture and the buttermilk, and mix until the batter is smooth, scraping the bowl down occasionally. Use a spatula to gently fold in the blueberries.

4. Fill the three cake pans evenly with the batter, and bake for 20 to 25 minutes, or until a toothpick stuck into the center comes out clean. Set aside on a wire rack to cool completely before removing from the pans.

5. *To build the cake,* spread some of the frosting over the layers, and stack the layers; then frost the sides of the cake.

Vegan Orange Cake

{ MAKES ONE 8-INCH
ROUND CAKE }

CAKE

2¼ cups all-purpose flour

1½ cups turbinado sugar

1½ teaspoons baking soda

¾ teaspoon kosher salt

1½ cups freshly squeezed
orange juice

1½ tablespoons freshly grated
orange zest

½ cup vegetable oil

1½ tablespoons apple cider vinegar

1½ teaspoons pure vanilla extract

ORANGE GLAZE

1 tablespoon freshly grated
orange zest

¼ cup freshly squeezed orange juice

1 cup confectioners' sugar

OUR VEGAN CLIENTELE LOVED to come in for food and tea, but missed getting to have dessert with their non-vegan friends. So we came up with this zesty cake, with an orange glaze that's so good even non-vegans have fallen for it!

1. *To make the cake*, preheat the oven to 350°F. Spray a deep 8-inch round nonstick cake pan with cooking spray. (If your pan is not nonstick, coat it with cooking spray and then line the bottom with parchment paper. This batter is extremely sticky!)

2. In a large mixing bowl, combine the flour, sugar, baking soda, and salt.

3. In a medium bowl, combine the orange juice and zest, oil, vinegar, and vanilla. Using a mixer or by hand, add the wet ingredients to the dry ingredients and mix until the batter is completely smooth.

4. Pour the batter into the prepared cake pan, and bake for 25 to 30 minutes, or until a toothpick stuck into the center comes out clean. Transfer the cake, still in the pan, to a wire rack to cool.

5. When it is cool, carefully remove the cake from the pan and place it on a cake plate or stand.

6. *To make the orange glaze*, whisk all the ingredients together in a medium bowl until the consistency is thick and smooth. Cover until ready to use.

7. Slowly pour the orange glaze onto the center of the cake so that it spreads evenly across the top and down the sides, covering the cake in a yummy, gooey glaze. Let the cake stand for at least 30 minutes to give the glaze a chance to set.

Vegan German Chocolate Cake

{ MAKES ONE 8-INCH
2-LAYER CAKE }

CAKE

3½ cups all-purpose flour

4 teaspoons baking powder

2 teaspoons baking soda

1 teaspoon kosher salt

2 cups soy milk

1½ cups unsweetened cocoa powder
   (we recommend Hershey's)

1 cup canola oil

3 cups real maple syrup

1 teaspoon distilled white vinegar

1 teaspoon pure vanilla extract

COCONUT-PECAN FROSTING

½ cup soy milk

¼ cup cornstarch

1 pinch kosher salt

2 cups firmly packed dark
   brown sugar

1½ cups coconut milk

2 teaspoons pure vanilla extract

3 cups sweetened shredded coconut

1 cup pecans, coarsely chopped

EVEN THE MOST PASSIONATE German chocolate cake lover will love this rich, dark vegan treat. It's sweetened mostly with maple syrup and loaded with dark chocolate. You won't miss the dairy at all, we promise. . . .

1. *To make the cake,* preheat the oven to 350°F. Have ready two 8-inch round nonstick cake pans.

2. In a large bowl, sift together the flour, baking powder, baking soda, and salt.

3. Heat the soy milk in a small saucepan to slightly bubbling, and then add the cocoa powder. Remove from the heat and whisk well.

4. In a medium bowl, combine the oil, maple syrup, vinegar, and vanilla. Whisk well. Pour in the soy milk–cocoa mixture, and whisk until smooth.

5. Using a mixer or by hand, add the wet ingredients to the dry ingredients and mix until the batter is smooth.

6. Pour the batter evenly into the two cake pans, and bake for 25 to 30 minutes, or until a toothpick stuck into the center comes out clean. Set the cake aside to cool thoroughly.

7. *To make the coconut-pecan frosting,* whisk the soy milk, cornstarch, and salt together in a small bowl.

8. In a medium saucepan over medium heat, dissolve the brown sugar in the coconut milk. Cook, whisking, until the mixture comes to a boil. Then reduce the heat to low and cook for 5 minutes, or until slightly thickened.

½ cup soy milk

8 ounces unsweetened chocolate

¼ cup real maple syrup

9. With the mixture on the stove still over low heat, pour in the soy milk mixture and stir continuously until the mixture is very thick and smooth. Remove from the heat and beat in the vanilla, coconut, and pecans. Cool before using.

10. *To make the chocolate ganache*, combine all the ingredients in a saucepan over low heat, and stir continuously until the glaze is smooth. Remove from the heat, stir for another 2 minutes, and then cool to room temperature.

11. *To build the cake*, place 1 cake layer on a cake plate or stand, and spread a layer of the coconut-pecan frosting over the top (but not the sides). Place the second layer on top of the first, and spread a very hearty layer of the frosting over the top. Using an offset spatula, ice the sides of the cake with a thick layer of ganache. Then warm about ¼ cup of the ganache in a small saucepan, or in a microwave oven, and drizzle it across the top of the cake (or use a pastry bag to pipe it).

Vanilla Cake with Chocolate Buttercream

{ MAKES ONE 8-INCH 3-LAYER CAKE }

WE MUST HAVE SPENT a year getting this one just right, so it was as moist as its chocolate counterpart and the chocolate buttercream was just chocolatey enough—not too overpowering. Well, we're proud to say we did it!

CAKE

2¼ cups all-purpose flour

2¼ teaspoons baking powder

¾ teaspoon kosher salt

1½ sticks (¾ cup) unsalted butter, at room temperature

1½ cups sugar

3 eggs

¾ teaspoon pure vanilla extract

¾ cup whole milk

CHOCOLATE FROSTING

2 sticks (1 cup) unsalted butter, at room temperature

3 tablespoons light corn syrup

½ teaspoon pure vanilla extract

2 cups confectioners' sugar

½ cup plus 6 tablespoons unsweetened cocoa powder

½ cup heavy cream, or more if needed

Fin with buttercream frosting

1. *To make the cake*, preheat the oven to 350°F. Have ready three 8-inch nonstick cake pans.

2. In a medium bowl, sift the flour, baking powder, and salt together.

3. In a large bowl, use a mixer to cream the butter and sugar until light and fluffy. Add the eggs, one at a time, mixing after each addition. Then add the vanilla, and mix until smooth. With the mixer set to the lowest speed, add the dry mixture a little at a time, alternating with the milk. Scrape down the mixing bowl after every addition and mix just until all is smooth, no more.

4. Fill the cake pans evenly with the batter, and bake for 20 to 25 minutes, or until a toothpick stuck into the center comes out clean. Set the pans on a wire rack to cool the cakes completely before frosting.

5. *To make the frosting*, use a mixer to cream the butter in a large bowl. Add the corn syrup and vanilla, and mix until smooth. With the mixer set on the lowest speed, gradually add the confectioners' sugar and the cocoa powder, alternating with the heavy cream. Scrape down the bowl and continue mixing until the frosting is consistent and smooth. Add a little bit more heavy cream if needed to get the right texture.

6. *To build the cake*, frost all three layers and stack them. Then frost the sides.

Red Velvet Cupcakes with Cream Cheese Frosting

{ MAKES 12 CUPCAKES }

WE DIDN'T REALLY KNOW anything about red velvet cupcakes when Sue started making them, but she assured us it was a big thing in the South. Of course we soon noticed them everywhere (once again, Sue was right!). Sue is generous with the cocoa in the batter, and the cream cheese frosting is just tart enough to cut some of the incredible sweetness of the moist cake. Kids love red velvet cupcakes—is it the red? Who knows?

1¾ cups all-purpose flour

¼ cup unsweetened cocoa powder (we recommend Hershey's)

¾ teaspoon kosher salt

1 cup vegetable oil

1¾ cups sugar

2 eggs

¼ cup plus 3 tablespoons red food coloring

¾ teaspoon pure vanilla extract

½ cup plus 2 tablespoons buttermilk

1 teaspoon baking soda

1¼ teaspoons distilled white vinegar

Cream Cheese Frosting (page 133)

1. Preheat the oven to 350°F.

2. In a medium bowl, sift the flour, cocoa powder, and salt together.

3. In a large bowl, use a mixer to beat the oil and sugar on medium speed until mixed. Add the eggs, one at a time, and mix until smooth. Add the food coloring and vanilla, and mix until the color is consistent throughout.

4. With the mixer set at the lowest speed, gradually add the dry ingredients, alternating with the buttermilk, and mix until the batter is smooth. Then add the baking soda and vinegar at the same time, and mix until fully incorporated.

5. Fill a nonstick muffin pan or 12 cupcake cups half-full with batter, and bake for 20 to 25 minutes, or until a toothpick inserted into the middle comes out clean. Set aside to cool completely in the pan.

6. Use an offset spatula to frost the cupcakes with cream cheese frosting. (For neater cupcakes, you can put the frosting in a pastry bag and pipe it onto the tops.)

Mint Black Bottom Cupcakes

{ MAKES 12 CUPCAKES }

2 teaspoons Trafalgar Square tea leaves (see Resources)

8 ounces cream cheese, at room temperature

1 egg

1⅓ cups sugar

½ teaspoon mint extract

5 to 7 drops green food coloring

1 cup mini chocolate chips

1½ cups all-purpose flour

¼ cup unsweetened cocoa powder (we recommend Hershey's)

1 teaspoon baking soda

¼ teaspoon salt

1 cup water

⅓ cup canola oil

1 tablespoon distilled white vinegar

1 teaspoon pure vanilla extract

WE GREW UP EATING only Junior Mints when we went to the movies because they were, according to our mom, the "healthiest of the movie candies" (don't ask). And thus started our love of mint and chocolate. These cupcakes have all the deliciousness of the classic black bottom cake with the plus of mint extract and our very own Trafalgar Square tea mix. If you're a fan of mint, these are your dream come true.

1. Preheat the oven to 350°F.

2. In a coffee or spice grinder, grind the tea leaves to a fine powder. Set aside.

3. In a large bowl, use a mixer to beat the cream cheese, egg, and ⅓ cup of the sugar until smooth and creamy. Add the mint extract and food coloring, and mix until the color is uniform throughout. Fold in the chocolate chips by hand, and set aside.

4. In a separate large bowl, combine the flour, cocoa powder, tea, baking soda, salt, and remaining 1 cup sugar. Make a well in the center and add the water, oil, vinegar, and vanilla. Mix well by hand until the mixture is smooth.

5. Fill a nonstick muffin pan or 12 cupcake cups one-third full of the chocolate batter, and then put a dollop of the green cream cheese batter on top of each. Bake for 20 to 25 minutes, or until a toothpick stuck into the middle comes out clean. Set aside to cool completely in the pan.

Chocolate Chai Cupcakes

{ MAKES 12 CUPCAKES }

CUPCAKES

3 teaspoons Indian Chai tea leaves (see Resources)

¾ cup all-purpose flour

2 tablespoons unsweetened cocoa powder (we recommend Hershey's)

¾ teaspoon baking powder

1 pinch kosher salt

4 ounces unsweetened chocolate

1¾ sticks (14 tablespoons) unsalted butter

1¼ cups sugar

4 eggs

> ✦ *Tip* ✦
>
> Chai tea is a great tea to bake and cook with because it adds a spicy character but isn't too strong for most people's palates.

THE CHAI TEA in these cupcakes is really evident and adds a ton of natural zest to the batter and frosting. They're delicious served with glasses of ice-cold milk.

1. *To make the cupcakes,* preheat the oven to 350°F.

2. In a coffee or spice grinder, grind the tea leaves to a powder.

3. Sift the flour, cocoa powder, baking powder, powdered tea, and salt into a medium bowl, and set it aside.

4. Make a water bath by filling a saucepan one-third full of water and bringing it to a simmer (you can use a double boiler). Set a Pyrex bowl over the saucepan, add the chocolate and butter to the bowl, and heat until they have melted, stirring gently to combine. Remove the bowl from the heat and stir in the sugar. Let cool for 10 minutes. Then place the mixture in a large bowl and use a mixer to beat it for 3 minutes, or until smooth. While still mixing, add the eggs, one at a time. Set the mixer at the lowest setting and add the dry ingredients, a little bit at a time, mixing until the batter is well blended and smooth.

5. Fill a nonstick muffin pan or 12 cupcake cups half-full with batter, and bake for 15 to 20 minutes, or until a toothpick stuck into the middle comes out clean. Set aside to cool completely in the pan.

CHAI SPICE BUTTERCREAM

1½ teaspoons Indian Chai tea
   leaves (see Resources)

1 stick (½ cup) unsalted butter,
   at room temperature

2½ cups confectioners' sugar

1 teaspoon ground ginger

½ teaspoon unsweetened cocoa
   powder (we recommend
   Hershey's)

2 tablespoons milk, or more
   if needed

¼ teaspoon pure vanilla extract

6. *To make the buttercream,* use a coffee or spice grinder to grind the tea leaves to a powder.

7. In a large bowl, use a mixer to cream the butter. Then slowly add the confectioners' sugar, powdered tea, ginger, and cocoa powder, alternating with the milk and vanilla. Mix until the buttercream is thoroughly smooth and combined. Use extra milk as needed, but be careful not to add too much, or the icing will be too soft.

8. Use an offset spatula to frost the cupcakes with the buttercream. (For neater cupcakes, you can put the frosting in a pastry bag and pipe it onto the tops.)

*Marlo gets a cupcake
from Melissa*

Banana Cupcakes with Cream Cheese Frosting

{ MAKES 12 CUPCAKES }

2 very ripe bananas

¾ cup canola oil

1 cup sugar

2 eggs

½ teaspoon pure vanilla extract

1 cup all-purpose flour

1 teaspoon baking soda

¼ teaspoon kosher salt

Cream Cheese Frosting (page 133)

LAUREN SWEARS THAT there's no bad day that can't be turned around with this bit of yum: a moist banana cupcake topped off with heavenly cream cheese frosting. Don't be afraid to use a heavy hand with the frosting—it's so good! But these cupcakes are great even unfrosted.

1. Preheat the oven to 350°F.

2. Mash the bananas in a small bowl, and set it aside.

3. In a large bowl, use a mixer to combine the oil and sugar until fully mixed. Add the eggs, one at a time, and then the vanilla, and keep mixing until smooth. Combine the flour, baking soda, and salt in a medium bowl. With the mixer set at the lowest speed, add the flour mixture a little at a time, mixing until all is combined and the batter is smooth. Use a spatula to fold in the bananas by hand.

4. Fill a nonstick muffin pan or 12 cupcake cups half-full with batter, and bake for 15 to 20 minutes, or until a toothpick stuck into the middle comes out clean. Set aside to cool completely in the pan.

5. Use an offset spatula to frost the cupcakes with the cream cheese frosting. (For neater cupcakes, you can put the frosting in a pastry bag and pipe it onto the tops.)

Oreo Cupcakes

{ MAKES 12 CUPCAKES }

Batter for Chocolate Cake
(page 126)

2 cups Marshmallow Fluff

10 to 12 Oreo cookies, crushed
into large chunks

The Yummiest Vanilla Buttercream
Frosting (page 129)

THIS IS THE CREATION of one of our bakers, Betina (thank you, Betina!). Our mother is such a health nut that if you offered her an actual Oreo, she would look at you as if you were crazy. But Michael gave her a box of these cupcakes for her birthday, and she ate every one! We take a rich chocolate cupcake, slice off the top, add a dollop of Marshmallow Fluff that literally soaks into the cake, put the top back on, and then frost it with buttercream frosting studded with chopped Oreos. It's a sweets lover's dream food.

1. Preheat the oven to 350°F.

2. Fill a nonstick muffin pan or 12 cupcake cups half-full with the batter, and bake for 15 to 20 minutes, or until a toothpick stuck into the middle comes out clean. Set aside to cool completely in the pan.

3. Use a paring knife to scoop a ½-inch-deep cap off the top of each cupcake. Set the tops aside; you will need them in a minute!

4. Use a melon baller to deposit a heaping scoop of Marshmallow Fluff into the center of each cupcake. Set the tops back on the cupcakes.

5. Use a spatula to gently fold the Oreos into the frosting. Using an offset spatula, carefully frost each cupcake with a very hearty amount of the Oreo frosting. Seriously, we're not kidding—don't hold back!

John making Oreo Cupcakes

Chocolate Pumpkin Cupcakes

{ MAKES 12 TO 18 CUPCAKES }

CUPCAKES

3 cups all-purpose flour

1 cup plus 2 tablespoons
   unsweetened cocoa powder
   (we recommend Hershey's)

4 teaspoons baking powder

2 teaspoons baking soda

1 teaspoon kosher salt

3 sticks (1½ cups) unsalted butter,
   at room temperature

2 cups granulated sugar

2 cups firmly packed dark brown
   sugar

6 whole eggs

2 egg yolks

4 teaspoons pure vanilla extract

1 cup buttermilk

2 cups canned pumpkin puree
   (all pumpkin, not pumpkin
   pie filling)

WE'RE FANS OF pumpkin—it's no secret—and it's largely due to our father's influence. He would try anything once, and something like pumpkin spread with cheese on bread was a no-brainer for him. (He insisted once that chocolate-dipped sardines *must* be good.) For these cupcakes, adding pumpkin to the rich chocolatey batter gives both immense flavor and extra moistness. But the *pièce de résistance* is the pumpkin–cream cheese frosting, which is extremely fluffy and yummy!

1. *To make the cupcakes,* preheat the oven to 350°F.

2. Sift the flour, cocoa powder, baking powder, baking soda, and salt into a large bowl and set aside.

3. In a separate large bowl, use a mixer to cream the butter and sugars until light and fluffy. With the mixer running, add the eggs and the egg yolks, one at a time, and then add the vanilla. With the mixer on its lowest setting, alternate adding the dry ingredients with the buttermilk until all of the ingredients are fully combined. Add the pumpkin and mix until the batter is smooth and consistent.

4. Fill one or two nonstick muffin pans, or 12 to 18 cupcake cups, half-full with batter, and bake for 20 to 25 minutes, or until a toothpick stuck into the middle comes out clean. Set aside to cool completely in the pan.

PUMPKIN-CREAM CHEESE FROSTING

1 stick (½ cup) unsalted butter, at room temperature

12 ounces (1½ cups) cream cheese, at room temperature

4 cups confectioners' sugar

1 teaspoon ground cinnamon

¼ teaspoon ground nutmeg

¾ cup canned pumpkin puree (all pumpkin, not pumpkin pie filling)

5. *To make the frosting,* use a mixer to cream the butter and cream cheese in a large bowl until fully combined and smooth. With the mixer on its lowest setting, slowly add the confectioners' sugar, cinnamon, and nutmeg, and mix until all is incorporated and smooth. Add the pumpkin puree and mix until you have a light, smooth frosting.

6. Use an offset spatula to frost the cupcakes. (For neater cupcakes, you can put the frosting in a pastry bag and pipe it onto the tops.)

Outside Chapter III

Other Sweets and Treats
for the Alice in All of Us

＋ ＊ ＋

As if cake and cupcakes and cookies weren't temptation enough, there have to be even more ways to satisfy the sweet tooth: the dessert beverage, the s'more (which can't even be put in a category—I mean, it requires an open fire, for heaven's sake!). Isn't life good? Even something as innocent-sounding as banana bread can take on a whole new meaning when you've taken a bite of something truly special. Really, why stop anywhere? When you can have your chocolate, coconut, and pecans all in one bar, why not go ahead and do it? Why not make a curd from naturally delicious fruit? Like all things yummy, the "other" dessert always blends two flavors at the very least into one masterpiece. (And of course, tea is one of those flavors for us whenever possible!)

"I ran in out of the cold . . . and there was beautiful Lauren! 'Lauren,' I asked, 'do you have hot chocolate?' 'Oh yes, we do. Delicious, too!' I decided to partake in a cup. Then she asked the magic question: 'Do you want spices in it to make it hot?' Oh my, that's right up my alley! Hot chocolate that's not only hot but HOT, with spices like cayenne pepper and such! It took a little bit of time because every cup is made to order, and then it appeared . . . steaming hot. I couldn't wait to try it! It was delicious! So good you might even say it's lethal because . . . you will want it ALL the time! So one day if you are coming in out of the cold . . . try it, there is nothing like it! Alice's Tea Cup Hot Chocolate. Treat yourself!"
—Bernadette Peters

Maddan, happy with his tea and cake!

Alice's Cocoa Loco

{ MAKES 4 TO 6 SERVINGS }

¾ cup unsweetened Valrhona cocoa
  powder or other premium
  unsweetened cocoa powder

1 cup turbinado sugar

¼ teaspoon ground cinnamon

¼ teaspoon ground nutmeg

¼ teaspoon cayenne pepper (less
  if you're sensitive to heat!)

2 cups milk

2 cups heavy cream

3 to 5 tablespoons cornstarch
  (depending on how thick you
  want your cocoa to be)

THIS COCOA IS THICK, kind of like melted fudge in a cup. The cayenne sneaks up on you, but in the best way possible. *¡Muy caliente!* Use Valrhona cocoa powder if you can, but this cocoa will be amazingly decadent no matter what. You can add a dollop of whipped cream or some marshmallows if you like, but we prefer it on its own, as it's incredibly rich.

1. Combine the cocoa powder, sugar, and spices in a medium bowl and set it aside.

2. In a large saucepan over low heat, heat the milk and cream to almost boiling. Take care that the mixture does not scorch. Whisk in the dry mixture until there are no lumps.

3. In a small bowl, add the cornstarch to ¼ cup cold water and stir until fully dissolved. Slowly whisk the cornstarch mixture into the hot cocoa, whisking constantly until the cocoa starts to thicken a lot.

4. Pour the cocoa into mugs and serve immediately!

Maddan and Ava having cocoa

Sue's Magical Banana Bread

{ MAKES 2 LOAVES }

7 very ripe bananas

3 cups sugar

2¼ cups vegetable oil

5 eggs

3¾ cups all-purpose flour

3 teaspoons baking soda

2 teaspoons ground cinnamon

2 teaspoons kosher salt

WE STARTED MAKING banana bread to do something special for kids in our peanut butter and jelly sandwiches (see page 101), but honestly, the banana bread was just *too* good not to serve it on its own as well. Warm a slice for a more decadent snack, bake it for a little crispy texture, spread some butter or preserves on it, or simply enjoy it in its birthday suit straight out of the oven! (Well, let it cool a little first.)

1. Preheat the oven to 325°F, and lightly butter and flour two loaf pans or use nonstick ones.

2. Mash the bananas well in a medium bowl. Set it aside.

3. In a large bowl, use a mixer set on the lowest speed to combine the sugar, oil, and eggs. Don't whip them! Slowly add the flour, baking soda, cinnamon, and salt, scraping the sides of the bowl occasionally, and mix until all is fully incorporated. Use a spatula to fold in the mashed bananas by hand.

4. Pour the batter evenly into the two pans, and bake for 1 to 1½ hours, checking every 10 minutes after the first hour, until a toothpick inserted into the center of a loaf comes out clean. Let cool in the pans before slicing. Freeze the second loaf to enjoy later.

Indian-Spiced Chai Tea– Infused Crème Brûlée

{ MAKES 4 TO 6 SERVINGS }

2 cups heavy cream

⅜ cup plus ½ cup sugar

1½ teaspoons pure vanilla extract

3 tablespoons Indian Chai tea leaves (see Resources)

6 large egg yolks

THERE'S REALLY NO BAD tea infusion for crème brûlée. We knew from the moment we opened Alice's Tea Cup that we wanted a small crème brûlée as an option for our Mad Hatter tea services. We began with Earl Grey Crème Brûlée, moved to Cinnamon Spice Crème Brûlée for a while, and dabbled with a Rooibos Coconut Vanilla Crème Brûlée. They were *all* good. But the chai crème brûlée has stayed on our menu the longest, mostly because the chai tea provides the right spice and zestiness here—something that's usually not expected in a crème brûlée, but is very welcome. Experiment with your own favorite tea!

1. Preheat the oven to 325°F. Place four to six shallow crème brûlée ramekins in a 9 × 13-inch baking pan, and fill the pan with water up to half the height of the ramekins.

2. In a medium saucepan, combine 1 cup of the heavy cream, ⅜ cup of the sugar, the vanilla, and the tea leaves, and bring it to a boil over low heat. Pour the mixture through a strainer into a large bowl. Discard the strained tea leaves.

3. In a medium mixing bowl, thoroughly whisk the egg yolks into the remaining 1 cup heavy cream. Very slowly drizzle the egg mixture into the warm chai mixture, stirring constantly to keep the eggs from cooking.

4. Distribute the mixture evenly among the ramekins. Carefully set the pan with the ramekins in the oven, and cook for about 40 minutes, or until the sides of the custards are slightly darker but the centers are still a bit jiggly.

5. Take the ramekins out of the water bath, cover them in plastic wrap, and refrigerate them for at least 2 hours, until the custard has completely firmed.

6. When you're ready to caramelize the tops, let the ramekins come to room temperature, about 30 minutes. Sprinkle the remaining ½ cup sugar evenly over the tops of the custards. Using a kitchen torch, melt the sugar until it forms a hard sheet over the custard. Let the dishes sit for a few minutes, and then eat!

NOTE: Torches are available at Williams-Sonoma and other kitchenware stores.

✦ ✦ ✦

Hello Dolly Bars

{ MAKES 9 TO 12 BARS }

2 teaspoons Rooibos Admiral's Cup tea leaves (see Resources)

1 stick (½ cup) unsalted butter, melted

1 cup graham cracker crumbs

1 cup sweetened shredded coconut

1 cup dark chocolate chips

1 cup chopped pecans

One 14-ounce can sweetened condensed milk

HELLO, DOLLY. It *is* so nice to have you back where you belong: in my belly! These bars may have a fun name, but the true delight is in eating them—they're a blend of everything yummy. We infuse them with Rooibos Admiral's Cup tea for extra flavor! (Photograph on page 113.)

1. Preheat the oven to 325°F.

2. In a coffee or spice grinder, grind the tea leaves to a fine powder. Set aside.

3. Pour the butter into a 9 × 13-inch baking pan. Evenly layer the graham cracker crumbs, coconut, chocolate chips, and pecans in the pan. Sprinkle the tea powder across the top as evenly as possible. Drizzle the condensed milk evenly on top.

4. Bake for 25 to 30 minutes, or until the coconut is toasted and the chocolate chips are melted. Cool thoroughly in the pan before cutting into bars.

Alice'S'mores

{ MAKES I S'MORE }

2 Graham Cracker Cookies
(recipe follows)

2 ice cream scoops Marshmallow
Fluff

2 ice cream scoops White Rabbit
Dark Chocolate Mousse
(page 166)

½ cup Chocolate Sauce (recipe
follows)

½ teaspoon confectioners' sugar

John making Alice'S'mores

EVEN ADULTS WILL DELIGHT in these, and not only for reasons of nostalgia. Using Marshmallow Fluff, our amazing chocolate mousse, and homemade graham crackers—and let's not forget the torch!—this dessert combines a wonderful list of stand-alone favorites while also managing to look pretty impressive on a dish. Because the chocolate mousse is so chocolatey and pure, adults will feel as if they're eating a gourmet dessert, even if it does bring back some campfire memories . . .

Place one of the cookies on a plate with ½ teaspoon of the Marshmallow Fluff underneath it to keep it in from shifting on the plate. Place an ice cream scoop of chocolate mousse on top of the cookie. Place a scoop of Fluff on top of the mousse. Using a kitchen torch, fire the top of the Fluff until it is browned (not burned). Place the other cookie on top of the fired Fluff, add another scoop of chocolate mousse and another scoop of Fluff, and again use the torch to brown the top of the Fluff. Drizzle the chocolate sauce across the top, and sprinkle with the confectioners' sugar. Eat immediately!

GRAHAM CRACKER COOKIES

{ MAKES 10 TO 12 COOKIES }

3 cups graham cracker crumbs

1 cup all-purpose flour

½ cup confectioners' sugar

½ cup firmly packed dark brown sugar

2 teaspoons baking powder

2 teaspoons ground cinnamon

2 sticks (1 cup) unsalted butter, at room temperature

⅓ cup milk

1. Preheat the oven to 350°F.

2. In a large bowl, combine the graham cracker crumbs, flour, sugars, baking powder, and cinnamon. Add the butter and use a mixer to combine until crumbly and well incorporated. Slowly add the milk, mixing until the dough is combined and fairly wet. Cover with plastic wrap and refrigerate for at least 1 hour, until firm.

3. Roll the dough out on a floured surface to about ¼-inch thickness. Use a 3½-inch biscuit cutter (with or without scalloped edges) to cut the dough into rounds. Remove the surrounding dough, wrap it, and refrigerate until you're ready to make the next batch. Lift the dough rounds with an offset spatula and place them on a nonstick baking sheet.

4. Bake for 12 to 14 minutes, or until they are brown (they should be crispy, not chewy).

5. Cool on a wire rack. Store in an airtight container for up to a week.

CHOCOLATE SAUCE

{ MAKES JUST OVER 1 CUP, ENOUGH FOR 4 TO 6 SMORES, OR ENJOY IT OVER ICE CREAM }

8 ounces dark chocolate pistoles or quality semisweet chocolate (see Note)

⅜ to ½ cup heavy cream

1. Melt the chocolate in a small bowl in a microwave oven at 1-minute intervals, stirring after each interval so it doesn't burn. (If you don't have a microwave, use a double boiler or place the ingredients in a heat-proof measuring cup or bowl set inside a saucepan filled halfway with water, and bring the water to a simmer over medium heat; stir occasionally until the chocolate has melted.)

2. Whisking constantly, drizzle ⅜ cup of the heavy cream into the melted chocolate, adding a little more cream as needed to get the chocolate sauce to your desired consistency.

NOTE: We recommend Cacao Barry Dark "Favorites Mi-Amère" Pistoles if you can get them. If not, Baker's Semi-Sweet Chocolate will also work.

White Rabbit Dark Chocolate Mousse

{ MAKES 6 TO 8 SERVINGS }

9 ounces dark chocolate pistoles or quality semisweet chocolate (see Note)

1½ teaspoons Medaglia D'Oro instant espresso powder, dissolved in 2 tablespoons hot water

2½ cups heavy cream

5 egg whites (the eggs will not be cooked, so if there's any concern about food safety, please use pasteurized eggs)

⅓ cup sugar

ALICE WOULD BE PROUD of our clever naming of this decadent dessert because we don't use white chocolate in it; we're simply tipping our hat to that tardy rabbit. The mousse is the key ingredient for our s'mores recipe, but so wonderful just by itself! Lauren's best friend, Mishna, considers this one a *must* at every visit to the Tea Cup!

1. Melt the chocolate in a small bowl in a microwave oven at 1-minute intervals, stirring after each interval so it doesn't burn. (If you don't have a microwave, use a double boiler or place the ingredients in a heat-proof measuring cup or bowl set inside a saucepan filled halfway with water, and bring the water to a simmer over medium heat; stir occasionally until the chocolate has melted.)

2. While the chocolate is melting, use a mixer to whip the espresso and cream in a large bowl until you have whipped cream, but don't overwhip. Set it aside.

3. In a separate bowl, use the mixer (with clean beaters) to whip the egg whites until they start to look white and creamy. Then add the sugar and whip just to combine. Again, do not overwhip!

4. When the chocolate is fully melted, pour it into a large mixing bowl. Add a scoop of the whipped cream and a scoop of the egg whites, and stir them thoroughly into the chocolate. In small alternating batches, fold the remaining whipped cream and egg whites into the chocolate until the mousse is smooth and even.

5. Cover and chill for at least an hour to set. If serving as a dessert (and not in the s'more's), first evenly divide the mousse among ramekins or parfait glasses; then cover and chill before serving.

NOTE: We recommend Cacao Barry Dark "Favorites Mi-Amère" Pistoles if you can get them. If not, Baker's Semi-Sweet Chocolate will also work.

Warm Soft Chocolate Cake

{ MAKES 4 SERVINGS }

1 stick (½ cup) salted butter

4 ounces bittersweet chocolate pistoles or morsels

2 whole eggs

2 egg yolks

¼ cup sugar

1 tablespoon all-purpose flour, plus more for dusting

Optional garnishes/serving ideas: confectioners' sugar, crème anglaise (page 46), whipped cream and berries, vanilla (or your favorite) ice cream

WE CREATED THIS LITTLE warm explosion of oozy chocolate goodness because we're chocolate fanatics and insisted on having a rich, chocolatey dessert on our menu to complement some of our fuller-bodied black teas and dessert blends. Mission accomplished! A few tea suggestions: Phoenix Dessert Blend (black tea flavored with honey, caramel, and vanilla), Symphony (black tea flavored with chocolate and strawberries), or a straight, rich Assam, such as Sessa.

1. Preheat the oven to 350°F. Spray four individual 4-ounce aluminum baking cups (not cupcake liners) with cooking spray or coat them with butter. Then dust them with flour. (This will help the cakes slide right out.)

2. In a medium glass bowl, melt the butter and chocolate in a microwave oven or in a water bath or double boiler. Mix thoroughly until you have a shiny chocolate sauce.

3. In a large bowl, use a mixer to beat the eggs, egg yolks, and sugar until thick. Add the chocolate/butter mixture and beat until thick. With the mixer running, add the 1 tablespoon flour.

4. Divide the mixture evenly among the prepared baking cups, and bake for 11 minutes. Watch the time carefully!

5. Turn each container upside down onto the center of a serving plate, and slowly lift and slightly shake the aluminum cup so that the cake slides out upside down. Serve with the garnish of your choice.

NOTE: You can prepare these ahead of time to bake later. Cover the filled baking cups and refrigerate for up to 3 days. Then bake the chilled cups for 13 minutes.

Queen of Tarts (French Vervain–Infused Lemon Tart)

{ MAKES 6 TO 8 TARTS }

2 cups all-purpose flour

¾ cup confectioners' sugar

1 pinch kosher salt

1 stick (½ cup) cold unsalted
    butter, cut into pieces

1 egg

French Vervain Lemon Curd
    (recipe follows)

THE OBVIOUS CHOICE of French Vervain to infuse our lemon curd struck Haley as a little blah—until she tried it. It added a ton of flavor, while the curd kept its amazing plump creaminess. This is one of those desserts that Haley's dear friend Maria always says she will just have one bite of and then finishes off in five minutes (hi, Maria!). Listen, can you blame her?

1. In a medium bowl, combine the flour, confectioners' sugar, and salt.

2. In a large bowl, use a mixer set on the lowest speed to cut the butter into the dry ingredients until the mixture resembles breadcrumbs. Add the egg and mix until all is incorporated and a workable dough is formed, but do not overknead the dough! Form the dough into a disk, wrap it in plastic, and refrigerate it for at least 1 hour.

3. When you're ready to bake the tart shells, preheat the oven to 400°F.

4. Divide the dough into enough equal portions to line six to eight 3½-inch tart pans. Lay a piece of parchment or wax paper on a flat surface, and set one of the dough portions on the paper. Put another piece of paper on top and use a rolling pin to roll out the dough, creating a round that is just a bit wider than the tart pan. Center the dough over the tart pan and lightly push it into the pan to form the tart shell, pinching the edges to make a scalloped design around the rim of the shell. Repeat with the rest of the dough.

5. Using a fork, perforate the bottom of each tart crust several times to keep them from puffing up while they bake. Place the tart pans on a large baking sheet, and bake for 10 to 12 minutes, or until the crusts are lightly browned.

Lori and Jessica zesting lemons

6. Move the baking sheet to a cooling rack and let cool completely before removing the shells from the pans. (You can store unused tart shells in an airtight container for up to a week.)

7. Once the shells have fully cooled, spoon 4 to 5 tablespoons of the curd into each shell. Use the back of the spoon to spread the curd, distributing it evenly inside the shell. These can be served as is or, if desired, garnished with anything from fresh berries to sprigs of mint!

FRENCH VERVAIN LEMON CURD

{ MAKES 4 TO 6 SERVINGS }

7 egg yolks

¾ stick (6 tablespoons) unsalted butter

Grated zest of 3 lemons

⅜ cup freshly squeezed lemon juice

½ cup plus 1 tablespoon sugar

2 tablespoons French Vervain tea leaves (see Resources)

THIS CURD IS ALSO amazing served with berries in our crepes (page 48)!

1. Whisk the egg yolks in a large bowl.

2. In a medium saucepan, combine the butter, lemon zest and juice, sugar, and tea leaves, and bring the mixture to a boil over low to medium heat. Strain the mixture into a medium bowl, discarding the zest, lemon pulp, and tea leaves.

3. While whisking constantly, slowly drizzle the juice mixture into the egg yolks, being very careful not to cook the yolks.

4. Fill a large bowl with ice and nestle a smaller bowl into the ice.

5. Return the mixture to the saucepan and cook, stirring constantly, over very low heat until it starts to thicken slightly, about 10 minutes. Do not allow the mixture to overheat or come to a simmer, or the eggs will scramble!

6. Pour the mixture into the smaller bowl nestled in the ice (this allows the curd to cool and thicken at the same time). Stir for 2 to 3 minutes, or until the mixture is the desired thickness. This will keep, wrapped, in the refrigerator for up to a week.

Mar-tea-nis

✦ ✦ ✦

It wasn't until we found our second location—which we call Chapter II—on East Sixty-fourth Street that we even thought of making cocktails with tea infusions, but the previous restaurant there had a liquor license, so why not? We sat down one day and dreamed up our "mar-tea-nis," which was a lot of fun, but not nearly as fun as testing them out! Mar-tea-nis are some of your favorite cocktails—turned on their ears, of course, with a complementary tea infusion to set them apart from the usual dreary cocktail offerings. We invite you to come up with your own wonderful combinations. Just don't be shy—share them with us (e-mail feedback@alicesteacup.com) so that we can serve them here, too! And if you do happen to drink enough to take a fall down the rabbit hole, don't get lost in Wonderland for the night!

CLOCKWISE FROM LEFT: *Alice's Peach Tea Bellini (page 183)*, *Rose Mélange Mar-tea-ni (page 174)*, *Mango Maté Mimosa (page 175)*, *and Alice's Tea-jito (page 176)*.

Rose Mélange Mar-tea-ni

{ MAKES 1 COCKTAIL }

*3 ounces premium vodka
(we recommend Ketel One)*

*1 ounce Rose Tea Mélange
Concentrate (recipe follows)*

*Rosebud from Rose Tea Mélange
(optional)*

ROSE TEA MÉLANGE
CONCENTRATE

*1 heaping tablespoon Rose
Tea Mélange tea leaves
(see Resources)*

THIS ELEGANT COCKTAIL is our twist on the traditional vodka martini. We give it just a bit of Rose Tea Mélange white tea for a subtle flavor that complements the vodka, but never competes.

1. Fill a cocktail shaker with ice. Add the vodka and Rose Tea Mélange Concentrate, cover, and shake vigorously.

2. Strain the liquid from the shaker into a chilled martini glass. Garnish with a rosebud from the dried tea for a touch of pretty!

Steep the tea in ¼ cup boiling-hot water for 3 minutes, then strain the tea, discarding the leaves. Refrigerate until cool. (Do not use in a cocktail until it has cooled completely.)

> **⋆ Tip ⋆**
> Be very sparing with the
> Rose Tea Mélange—a little
> goes a long way!

Mango Maté Mimosa

1 ounce Mango Maté Concentrate
(recipe follows)

1 ounce orange juice

3 ounces chilled champagne

THE MIMOSA IS SUCH a brunch staple, we simply had to have one, but we thought it would be magnificent with the addition of exotic Mango Maté! We were right. . . .

Pour the cooled Mango Maté Concentrate into a champagne flute. Add the orange juice. Top it off with the champagne. Stir well.

MANGO MATÉ CONCENTRATE

1 heaping tablespoon Mango Maté tea leaves (see Resources)

Steep the tea in ¼ cup boiling-hot water for 3 minutes. Then strain the tea, discarding the leaves. Refrigerate until cool. (Do not use in a cocktail until it has cooled completely.)

A party in progress
at Chapter I

Alice's Tea-jito

{ MAKES 1 COCKTAIL }

2 ounces white rum

2 ounces freshly squeezed lime juice

2 ounces Moroccan Mint Simple
　　Syrup (recipe follows)

1 fresh mint sprig, for garnish

1 splash seltzer

1 lime wedge, for garnish

OUR TAKE ON THE classic mojito gets its twist from Moroccan Mint tea. When we presented these for the first time at a certain jewelry designer's trunk sale, the universal response was "Oh, my!"

1. Fill a cocktail shaker with ice. Pour in the rum, lime juice, and mint syrup, cover, and shake vigorously.

2. Fill a tall glass with ice and add the mint sprig. Strain the liquid from the shaker into the glass, and top off with a splash of seltzer. Garnish with the lime wedge on the rim of the glass.

MOROCCAN MINT SIMPLE SYRUP

{ MAKES ENOUGH
FOR 4 DRINKS }

3 heaping tablespoons Moroccan
　　Mint tea leaves (see Resources)

1 cup sugar

Steep the tea leaves in 1 cup boiling-hot water for 3 minutes. Then strain the tea into a small bowl, discarding the leaves. Add the sugar and stir until it has completely dissolved. Refrigerate until cool. (Do not use the simple syrup in a cocktail until it has cooled completely.)

Berry Bunch Mar-tea-ni

{ MAKES 1 COCKTAIL }

3 heaping teaspoons Berry Bunch Tisane tea (see Resources)

2 ounces premium vodka

2 ounces white cranberry juice

1 lime or orange wedge, for garnish

IT'S HOT PINK, it's berry flavored, and it's not a Cosmo . . . need we say more? Okay, maybe just a little more: This delightful vodka-based martini includes our Berry Bunch fruit tisane for a tangy, sweet cocktail treat!

1. Steep the Berry Bunch Tisane tea in ¼ cup boiling-hot water for 7 minutes. Then strain the tea, discarding the fruit. Cover the tea and refrigerate until cool.

2. Fill a cocktail shaker with ice. Add the vodka, tea, and cranberry juice. Cover, and shake vigorously. Strain the liquid from the shaker into a chilled martini glass. Garnish with the lime or orange wedge on the rim of the glass.

Chai Me Up

{ MAKES I COCKTAIL }

2 heaping teaspoons Indian Chai
tea leaves (see Resources)

1½ ounces brandy

1 ounce Amaretto di Saronno
liqueur

½ ounce Frangelico liqueur

½ ounce Chai Milk (recipe follows)

1 pinch ground nutmeg

INDIAN CHAI TEA, with all its amazing zest, mixes with brandy, Amaretto di Saronno, and Frangelico to warm your insides a bit. But it is the chai milk that makes this more of a decadent dessert-like cocktail that looks amazing in your glass.

1. Steep the tea leaves in ¼ cup boiling-hot water for 3 minutes. Strain the tea, discarding the leaves, and cool it in the refrigerator.

2. Fill a cocktail shaker with ice. Add the brandy, liqueurs, chai tea, and Chai Milk. Cover, and shake vigorously. Strain the liquid from the shaker into a chilled martini glass. Garnish with a sprinkling of the nutmeg, and serve.

CHAI MILK

{ MAKES ENOUGH
FOR 16 DRINKS }

1 cup whole milk

3 tablespoons honey

In a small saucepan over low heat, warm the milk to hot but not boiling. Remove from the heat, stir in the honey, and chill before using in a cocktail. Store the remaining chai milk, covered, in the refrigerator for up to a week.

Ginger Mar-tea-ni

{ MAKES 1 COCKTAIL }

2 ounces Smirnoff grapefruit vodka

1 ounce Organic Ginger Tea
Simple Syrup (recipe follows)

1 ounce freshly squeezed lime juice

1 lime wedge, for garnish

ORGANIC GINGER TEA SIMPLE SYRUP

{ MAKES ENOUGH FOR
ABOUT 8 DRINKS }

4 heaping tablespoons Organic
Ginger tea (see Resources)

1 cup sugar

LAUREN DREAMED this one up for the same party where the Tea-jito was introduced. The host of the party found a vodka company to co-sponsor the event, and they sent over grapefruit vodka. This inspired Lauren to think, "Hmm . . . Organic Ginger tea and a splash of lime would make this vodka sing!" It did . . .

Fill a cocktail shaker with ice. Add the vodka, ginger syrup, and lime juice. Cover, and shake vigorously. Strain the liquid from the shaker into a chilled martini glass. Garnish with the lime wedge on the rim of the glass.

Steep the tea in 1 cup boiling-hot water for 7 minutes. Then strain the tea into a container, discarding the ginger pieces. Add the sugar and stir until it has dissolved. Chill thoroughly before using.

Outside Chapter II

Inspiration Julep

{ MAKES 1 COCKTAIL }

2 ounces Maker's Mark bourbon

2 ounces Inspiration Simple Syrup
(recipe follows)

1 fresh mint sprig, for garnish

INSPIRATION SIMPLE SYRUP

{ MAKES ENOUGH FOR
ABOUT 4 DRINKS }

4 heaping tablespoons Inspiration
tea leaves (see Resources)

1 cup sugar

WHO DOESN'T LOVE a julep on a hot summer day? This version replaces the muddled mint with our Inspiration tea (a blend of peppermint leaves, rose petals, and rose hips) for a julep that will leave you longing for summer, all year round . . .

Fill a cocktail shaker with ice. Add the bourbon and Inspiration syrup, cover, and shake vigorously. Fill a rocks glass with ice and add the mint sprig. Strain the liquid from the shaker into the glass, and serve.

Steep the tea leaves in 1 cup boiling-hot water for 7 minutes. Then strain the tea into a container, discarding the tea leaves. Add the sugar and stir until it has dissolved. Chill thoroughly before using.

Lavender Earl Grey Mar-tea-ni

{ MAKES 1 COCKTAIL }

2 heaping teaspoons Lavender Earl Grey tea leaves (see Resources)

2 ounces Bombay Sapphire gin

HALEY'S BRAINCHILD TAKES the gin martini to a new level of excitement and complexity. Who woulda thunk that gin, lavender, and Earl Grey tea would mix? Well, they sure do, and the result is divine . . .

1. Steep the tea leaves in ¼ cup boiling-hot water for 3 minutes. Strain the tea, discarding the tea leaves, and refrigerate until cool.

2. Fill a cocktail shaker with ice. Add the gin and the tea, cover, and shake vigorously. Strain the liquid from the shaker into a chilled martini glass.

◆ ◆ ◆

The Man's Drink

{ MAKES 1 COCKTAIL }

2 heaping teaspoons Lapsang Souchong Superior tea leaves (see Resources)

2 ounces Johnnie Walker Black Label blended Scotch

AS GIRLY AS WE may seem at Alice's Tea Cup, we pride ourselves on welcoming men as much as women, so we thought long and hard about what kind of tea drink would excite our male clientele. We thought, "Scotch is a man's drink, so why not combine it with a deeply smoky tea, like Lapsang Souchong, for that Scotch-and-cigar taste?" It worked, and men aren't the only ones who love this gem of a cocktail.

1. Steep the tea leaves in ¼ cup boiling-hot water for 3 minutes. Strain the tea, discarding the tea leaves, and refrigerate until cool.

2. Fill a rocks glass with ice, and add the Scotch and tea. Stir well.

Mauritius Storm

{ MAKES 1 COCKTAIL }

*2 heaping teaspoons Mauritius
tea leaves (see Resources)*

*2 ounces Myers's Original
Dark Rum*

½ ounce freshly squeezed lime juice

2½ ounces ginger ale

1 lime wedge, for garnish

EVER HAD A DARK 'N' STORMY? If you have, then you know how delicious they are. We wanted to create our own version with tea, and what better tea to do it with than Mauritius? Dark rum, Mauritius (black tea with a natural vanilla flavor), and ginger ale, with a wedge of lime. The trouble is, these go down *way* too smoothly . . .

1. Steep the tea leaves in ¼ cup boiling-hot water for 3 minutes. Strain the tea (we recommend using an all-cotton tea filter sock), discard the leaves, and refrigerate the tea until cool.

2. Fill a tall glass with ice and add the rum, tea, and lime juice. Top it off with the ginger ale, and stir well. Garnish with the lime wedge.

❖ ❖ ❖

Tequila Negra

{ MAKES 1 COCKTAIL }

*2 heaping teaspoons Black Fruits
tea leaves (see Resources)*

1 tablespoon honey

2 ounces Jose Cuervo Gold tequila

THINK SWEET TEQUILA on the rocks with a fruity twist. Our Black Fruits tea was the obvious choice here, because it gives depth to the tequila by adding a dark, robust, fruity flavor. Serve this one on the rocks!

1. Steep the tea leaves in ¼ cup boiling-hot water for 3 minutes. Strain the tea into a container, discarding the tea leaves. Stir in the honey, cover, and refrigerate until cool.

2. Fill a rocks glass with ice, and add the tea and the tequila. Stir well.

Alice's Peach Tea Bellini

{ MAKES I COCKTAIL }

1 ounce Peach Tea Simple Syrup
   (recipe follows)

1 teaspoon freshly squeezed
   orange juice

4 ounces chilled champagne

PEACH TEA SIMPLE SYRUP

{ MAKES ENOUGH
  FOR 8 DRINKS }

3 heaping tablespoons
   Peach Tea with Flowers leaves
   (see Resources)

1 cup sugar

OUR VERSION OF THE CLASSIC Bellini cocktail—
a little more complex, and even tastier, in our opinion!

Pour the peach syrup into a champagne flute, add the
orange juice, and top it off with the champagne. Stir well,
and serve.

Steep the tea leaves in 1 cup boiling-hot water for 3 minutes.
Then strain the tea into a container, discarding the tea leaves.
Add the sugar and stir until dissolved. Refrigerate until
completely cooled before using.

The Basics of Brewing Tea

✦ ✦ ✦

*L*et's not overcomplicate things. Yes, everyone likes their tea a bit different. Our mother, for example, might as well be drinking lighter fluid the way she brews her Sessa, while our father has forever brewed his tea with the textbook ratio of tea to water, and for only 3 minutes. Here are the general rules:

✦ For black tea, use 1 teaspoon tea per 8-ounce cup of 200°F water. Brew for only 3 minutes, or you'll get that bitter tannin flavor that we so kindly referred to above as lighter fluid.

✦ For green or white tea, use 1 teaspoon tea per 8-ounce cup of 180°F water. Brew for only 2 minutes, or you'll get that tannin flavor here as well.

✦ For all herbal tisanes and caffeine-free or decaffeinated teas, use 1 teaspoon tea per 8-ounce cup of 200°F water. Brew for 7 minutes, or longer to enjoy the health benefits of rooibos specifically. The tea will get stronger but not more bitter, because its tannin content is low.

Rachel making tea at Chapter II

And some brewing tips:

+ We recommend that you use all-cotton tea filter socks, which prevent any leaves from getting into the liquid, especially when you're brewing really fine teas such as fannings (including Cameroon Fannings, Mauritius, and African Dew) and rooibos. You can find tea filter socks on our website and at specialty stores.

+ You can reuse white and green tea bags for a second cup; they will maintain a fair amount of flavor if brewed for only the 2 minutes suggested.

*Dad brewing a pot of
Cameroon Fannings*

+ Don't get too worked up about the temperature of your water. A 20-degree difference is not going to ruin anything! If you don't own a thermometer, just bring your water to a boil (but don't overboil or you'll boil all the oxygen out of the water, which can make for bitter tea, believe it or not) and let it sit for 1 minute before adding it to the teapot or teacup.

If you know that you like stronger tea, double the amount per cup and see what you think. Or use less tea for a gentler flavor. You're the one who is going to drink it, after all.

Tea and Its Health Benefits

We're sure you've read ad nauseam about the health benefits of tea. Well, it's all true. And here's why:

Tea, which is to say the leaf that is known as *Camellia sinensis,* contains polyphenols, powerful antioxidants that are known to be cancer-fighting. Recent reports show that polyphenols may also reduce the risk of blood clotting, lower cholesterol, and reduce the risk of heart attacks. Green and white teas in particular are known for these benefits, because they are less processed.

For all you coffee drinkers out there, here's some info that might help you convert: Tea contains roughly half the caffeine of coffee. If you're thinking about switching from coffee to tea but can't imagine loving anything as "weak" as tea, just trust us and do a little test! Try substituting one of these teas for a few days: Mauritius, African Dew, Cameroon Fannings, or Maté Carnival. All are extremely potent teas with a deep brew, and all are great with milk.

Rooibos and other herbal "teas" come from an herb or flower instead of the tea plant, and they don't have the same particular health benefits as tea. Rooibos, or "Red Bush," from South Africa, does contain some antioxidants; it doesn't contain polyphenols. But it has been used for years to treat eczema and stomach and digestive problems (such as settling the stomachs of colicky babies). It's naturally caffeine-free, but it's known as a pick-me-up and a thirst quencher. It's rich in minerals such as calcium, fluoride, iron, potassium, magnesium, copper, sodium, and zinc, all of which are essential to the health and strength of your bones, skin, and teeth, and to your basic metabolic function, but it's low in tannins (which can negatively affect how your body absorbs iron and proteins). Haley once read that lukewarm brewed rooibos was a good topical solution to use for baby acne, and it worked like a miracle. Kids love the flavor of rooibos, even without any sweeteners—both Haley's children drank a bottle of it each night with a little rice milk. And, lastly, it is oxalic-acid-free, which means it can be freely consumed by people who suffer with kidney stones. I mean, could it be any better for you?

Herbal teas other than rooibos vary in specific health benefits and have tremendous calming effects—so enjoy your peppermint- or chamomile- or hibiscus-based "tea," and know that your body is thanking you in other, more subtle ways.

> **✦ Tip ✦**
>
> The more you brew rooibos, the more benefits you get from it, and because of the low tannin content, it won't turn bitter.

The Art of the Tea Party

✦ ✦ ✦

At Alice's, the most popular single thing on the menu (no, it's not the pumpkin scone) is our Mad Hatter afternoon tea. It's a full meal in afternoon tea form, which is to say that it's served on a three-tiered stand and will fully feed even the hungriest people. In fact, after every party, the partygoers leave with to-go boxes of food to sample at home. Of course we also have a lighter fare option, the Nibble, and a "hearty eater" plan called the Jabberwocky, which comes with unlimited sandwiches (we dare you . . .). Before we opened the first Alice's, Haley's husband, Michael, made a strong pitch that we needed to feed people thoroughly—none of this "tiny finger sandwich" or "petit four" stuff, which can have you skulking down the street for pizza after you've "enjoyed" high tea at a fancier establishment. Our sandwiches are cut into thirds and served on the middle tier, guarded by the scone tier at the top and the cake/cookie/tart/anything sweet tier at the bottom. This is decadence, comfort, and luxury on a three-tiered stand.

THROWING YOUR OWN TEA PARTIES

Our Mad Hatter is the centerpiece to our parties and makes them more festive and formal (not "black tie in a ballroom" formal, but "I am seriously throwing a party" formal). When it comes to throwing your own tea parties, you have a million options to choose from—décor, dress code, booze or no booze—but the easiest way to make a statement when you present your food is with a three-tiered afternoon tea stand.

Most people think of tea parties as prim, proper, pinky-up events, but we want tea parties to be

Sam with a Mad Hatter and tea stand

funky, fun, and whimsical—get that pinky down! We imagine our perfect tea party as an occasion to eat and drink heartily, and to laugh often. The key to a whimsical tea party is keeping it light and a bit edgy.

It's always fun to have a theme for a tea party, and here are some of our tried-and-true favorites from over the years. Or check out "Menu Pairings" on page 200, where we list of some our favorite food and drink combinations—lots of inspiration for your own party themes!

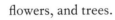
• *Tip* •

Formal (or informal) mailed invitations can be lovely, but a simple e-vite is almost always sufficient these days—you won't waste paper, and you can invest some of your creativity in the party itself! Bonus: Mother Nature will thank you.

A Garden Party

Ever since we opened the Caterpillar's Garden on the lovely shaded back porch at our Chapter III location on East Eighty-first Street, it's been in high demand. It's decorated with string lights, potted flowers, and two bright, colorful murals of *Alice in Wonderland*, and it has hosted everything from baby and bridal showers to birthday parties and our favorite: weddings! There's something so delightful about being outdoors with friends, surrounded by plants, flowers, and trees.

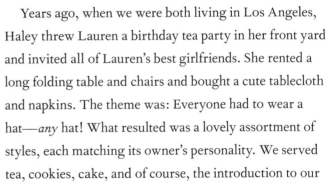

Years ago, when we were both living in Los Angeles, Haley threw Lauren a birthday tea party in her front yard and invited all of Lauren's best girlfriends. She rented a long folding table and chairs and bought a cute tablecloth and napkins. The theme was: Everyone had to wear a hat—*any* hat! What resulted was a lovely assortment of styles, each matching its owner's personality. We served tea, cookies, cake, and of course, the introduction to our scones. It was one of Lauren's favorite birthdays ever.

To throw your own garden tea party, all you need is your imagination. Check the Party Goods section on page 216 to find everything from string lights in any color your heart desires to

vibrant, happy-making oilcloths in whimsical (there's that word again) patterns sure to make any table smile. But remember: Be sure to plan carefully if you're having a garden party away from home, as carrying tons of food and tea in your heels can be challenging. Oh, and if the sun's a-shining, don't forget those hats!

Ladies Who Lunch

Have a bunch of great girlfriends? Have a desire to wear, *immediately*, that adorable new dress you just spent way too much on? Have a piece of gossip that absolutely needs to be shared straightaway? Then this is the perfect tea party for you! Here are the rules:

1. It's imperative to look stylish and fabulous.

2. Bright colors make all girls smile.

3. Leave your diets at the door—you can pick them up on the way out, but all girls need treats now and then. We believe beauty is all about balance, so don't come to a tea party unless you're willing to eat and drink to your heart's content!

4. Tea-infused cocktails are elegant, fun, and mighty tasty! Just be careful—those bright-colored "mar-tea-nis" will creep up on you . . .

5. This rule is of utmost importance: Gossip is wonderful, as long as it doesn't hurt anyone. If you're going to dish—and we *all* do—make sure you're not doing it at the expense of someone who might hear about it later.

6. Giggle often, laugh loudly, and make toasts throughout the event to honor each and every gal at the table!

A ladies' lunch at Chapter II

A few more suggestions: We highly recommend bright-colored décor to go with those pretty dresses and "mar-tea-nis." Flower string lights are one of our favorite decorations. And—listen up, ladies—we've never met a girl, no matter her age, who wasn't made happier by a few sparkles. Glitter is magical, and we girls need some magic once in a while.

Now that you have a blueprint for how to do it, call those "besties" and set a date. Pick the recipes you think they'll love the most, choose (or buy) the perfect dress, and decorate to your heart's content. And most important . . . be the hostess with the mostest!

Baby or Bridal Shower

When throwing a shower for a friend, all the same rules apply, but you can add another level to your fun: games! Now, a lot of women don't get that excited at the typical shower games, but we're not going to suggest that you take turns guessing the diameter of your expectant friend's waistline. We prefer things like Q&A games to see how well everyone knows the guest of honor (What's Susan's favorite movie?), passing around a sign-in book in which people can write their most profound (or profoundly funny) advice on marriage or babies . . . those kinds of games. Everyone loves to be the center of attention and have her girlfriends and family members fawn over her as if she has suddenly become the queen of some magical land, so go for it! Order or make that special cake that will reflect how well you know her. Fill the room with her favorite flower, hang lights or balloons in her favorite color—use your imagination! Give her favorite loose tea bagged inside a beautiful tea cup as a party favor! Even print your own labels and make your own friend-inspired brand named after her! But whatever you do, don't make a hat out of the gift ribbons and make her wear it. Really, is that ever a nice thing to do to someone?

Children's Tea Parties

These are some of our favorite parties—there's *so* much you can do, and it's so much fun to see children's faces when they enter a fairyland! First off: décor, décor, décor. Your party princess will most likely have a favorite theme, color, or even toy that you can center the party around. If there's a teddy bear she simply must sleep with every night, your theme could be "Bring a Bear to a Beary Special Party." If her favorite dress is covered in polka dots, throw a "Polka Palace Party." Or decorate a big box and fill it with dress-up clothes and hats and let your young (and older!) friends find a magical frock. You get the idea . . .

Once the theme has been decided, it's time to focus on the details—things like finding the perfect cookie cutters for the sandwiches (try twosmartcookies.com). Seriously, how fun would it be to have star-shaped sandwiches, or bear-shaped ones for your beary special tea party? Then choose your sweets: cake, cupcakes, cookies—all of the above? Next, pick an herbal tea or tisane (such as Berry Bunch Tisane, with its berry flavor and lovely pink color) that you can sweeten with some honey or agave (because even if your angel drinks unsweetened tea, there will be a guest who won't), and keep juice handy for those who won't even try the tea. Use china unless this party is for a three-year-old or younger— a child age four or older can handle it. You'll find that when children are wearing fairy wings and glitter and sitting down to tea, they bring out their most ladylike behavior.

Include your sweetie in making the decisions that count the most: who's invited, the theme, the colors,

A birthday party at Chapter I

what to use as a tablecloth (you can design your own with appliqués or patches), place cards and table settings (festive paper flowers and handmade bookmarks make great place cards). And whatever you do, don't forget the sparkle!

Now for the hard question: Entertainment or no entertainment? Do you need to hire a clown, or do you have an artistic friend who'd love the chance to do the face-painting? Perhaps someone could dress in character (how about Alice in Wonderland?) and lead the guests in song and dance. Or you could have the young ladies help you write a custom-tailored tea-party story—just write the first sentence and go guest by guest, asking each one to write the next sentence. What creative ideas will make those beautiful eyes sparkle and those cheeks lift in a smile? Only you know!

One last imperative note: Send each guest home with something, no matter how small— a tiara, a wand, bags of loose tea, or a little bottle of fairy dust number among our favorites. Sure, fairy dust may lead to an excessively sparkly home, but isn't true, unbridled happiness worth some vacuuming?

Décor Made Easy

We throw so many showers at Alice's, and we also cater at many homes, and we always get the same questions: "How do I decorate for a tea party?" and "What should I buy for the party?" The truth is, anything goes! You probably already have a ton of decorative elements in your house, so start there. Mix and match your cups, saucers, and plates (if you don't have enough, check out a local antique shop, or just buy lots from eBay). Use festively colored silk scarves over your tablecloth. Fill jars with bright marbles or painted shells or colorful feathers, or whatever you love. Hang those Christmas lights in July—Lauren has strings of colored lights hung in her apartment all year long! We prefer a whimsical, retro vibe with clean lines and bold colors (personally, we're not crazy about Victorian or Americana themes), but pretty much anything goes here, so let your creativity loose and do what speaks to you! If you've got it and it makes you happy, chances are it will make your guests happy, too.

Design your own tea party with what you already have at home

Menu Pairings

❖ ❖ ❖

*A*s you know by now, we're big on creativity and mix-and-match, but sometimes it's nice to have a menu plan in hand in case you want to focus on other elements of the party or gathering. Whether you're caffeine-free or full-octane, want to bake cookies or make a cake, are raring to include salad or simply want tea sandwiches, we have combos for you!

The Perfect Garden Party

Refreshing mint and citrus flavors mix perfectly with the clean flavors of these savory dishes. Add some richness and fruitiness in the desserts and you have the perfect outdoor fare that is flavorful but light!

MAR-TEA-NI: Alice's Tea-jito

TEAS: Rooibos Africana or Kimberly (rooibos), Energitea (green), Genmaicha (green), Castleton Estate (black), Sparrow's Soul (herbal)

SCONES: Chocolate Strawberry, Oatmeal

FARE: Lapsang Souchong Smoked Chicken Salad/Sandwich *or* Cucumber Watercress Sandwich

DESSERTS: Vegan Orange Cake, Mint Black Bottom Cupcakes

Autumn Leaves Party

As the weather gets colder, we start to crave richer, heartier fare. Chai spices, pumpkin flavors, rich chocolate, dark fruits, and intense savory sandwiches make this menu something your guests will remember for a very long time!

MAR-TEA-NI: Chai Me Up

TEAS: Indian Chai (black), Herbal Chai (rooibos), Empress Blend Rajini (black), Apricot Brandy (black)

SCONES: Mocha Chocolate Chip, Pumpkin, Banana Butterscotch

FARE: Cumin Carrot Sandwich, Alice's Croque Monsieur, Apple-Cinammon Butternut Squash Soup

DESSERTS: Warm Soft Chocolate Cake, Chocolate Cake with Vanilla Buttercream, Chocolate Pumpkin Cupcakes

Ladies Who Lunch Party

A perfect balance of clean citrus flavors, light, healthy sandwiches, and purifying teas makes this menu our go-to when we gather all the gals together!

MAR-TEA-NI: Ginger Mar-tea-ni

TEAS: Ginger Tea (black), Organic Ginger (tisane), Yerba Maté (maté), Drink-Me-Detox (rooibos, green, and white), Organic Snowbuds (white)

SCONES: Lemon Poppy Seed, Oatmeal, Lavender Earl Grey

FARE: Curried Chicken Sandwich, Maté Carnival Egg Salad Sandwich, Lapsang Souchong Smoked Chicken Salad/Sandwich, Thai Chickpea Soup

DESSERTS: Blueberry Lemon Cake, Queen of Tarts, Rooibos Africana Ranger Cookies

Her Perfect Shower Party

Mint and rose flavors mingle with berries and light, healthy fare. Oh, and there's a pink-and-green color scheme going on here that all are certain to notice and adore!

MAR-TEA-NI: Inspiration Julep

TEAS: Inspiration (herbal), Alice's Tea (black and green), Rose Tea Mélange (white)

SCONES: Mixed Berry, Berry Bunch Tisane–Infused

FARE: Cucumber Watercress Sandwich, Black Forest Ham and Gruyère Sandwich, Golden Afternoon Salad, Green Goddess Soup

DESSERTS: The Red Queen's Pink and White Chessboard Cookies, Thumbprint Cookies, Queen of Hearts Linzer Card Cookies, Red Velvet Cupcakes

Holiday Cheer Party

What does everyone think of when they hear the words "holiday fare"? Rich, bold flavors and traditional comfort foods. This menu will leave your guests feeling all warm and fuzzy inside . . .

MAR-TEA-NI: Mauritius Storm

TEAS: Mauritius (black), African Dew (black), Trafalgar Square (black), Christmas Tea (black), Christmas Brew (tisane)

SCONES: Cinnascone, Vanilla Bean, Peppermint Stick, Rice Krispies Treats, Turtle

FARE: Alice's Croque Madame, Warm Pear and Endive Salad, Warm Lentil Salad (with bacon), Rooibos Tomato Soup

DESSERTS: Carrot Cake, Double Chocolate Cookies, Alice'S'mores, Alice's Cocoa Loco

A Midsummer Night's Party

For those balmy summer evenings, we suggest these intense and slightly exotic flavors. Set a table outside, use Moroccan tea glasses with tea lights in them for mood lighting, and watch everyone feel instantly transported to a happy place . . .

MAR-TEA-NI: Tequila Negra

TEAS: Black Fruits (black), St. Mark (black), Hawaiian Paradise (tisane), Bianca (herbal)

SCONES: Berry Bunch Tisane–Infused, Buttermilk

FARE: Curried Chicken Sandwich, Alice's Hummus Sandwich, Warm Lentil Salad (without bacon)

DESSERTS: Banana Cupcakes with Cream Cheese Frosting, White Rabbit Dark Chocolate Mousse, Vegan German Chocolate Cake, Indian-Spiced Chai Tea–Infused Crème Brûlée

It's His Birthday Party!

We promise, this menu will make him think twice about tea fare being "girly"! Smoky flavors, hearty eats, and sinfully sweet desserts will have him wishing his birthday came more than once a year!

MAR-TEA-NI: The Man's Drink

TEAS: Lapsang Souchong Superior (black), Mt. Everest Breakfast (black), Sessa (black), Rooibos Phoenix (rooibos), Osmanthus Flower (herbal)

SCONES: Walnut Stilton, Bacon Cheddar, Banana Butterscotch

FARE: Alice's BLT, Alice's Burger, Alice's King Reuben, Warm Pear and Endive Salad, Turkey Chili

DESSERTS: Alice'S'mores, Banana Nutella Cake, Hello Dolly Bars, Rooibos Phoenix Oatmeal Butterscotch Chip Cookies

Tea-Dyeing Linens (and Clothes!)

◆ ◆ ◆

As you know, we're big tea advocates. Tea for drinking, tea for recipes, tea for health. But tea can also be used as a marvelous, subtle dye—a wonderful solution to graying whites or boring fabrics. When we started our tea-dyeing experiments, we dyed about two dozen linens for Alice's before deciding they were too amazing to use daily in the restaurant, where they would surely get stained in a nondeliberate way. But we do use them for our catered events and even parties in the restaurant upon request, and they always add a festive touch.

Try it at home yourself, and in only a couple of hours you can turn an ordinary tablecloth (or some napkins, or even clothes!) from new to beautifully aged. Follow the guidelines below, and let your muse run free!

1. Choose your item to dye.

Any fabric of 100% cotton or linen will soak up your tea "dye" in no time flat. But be sure that the fabric is 100% natural fibers—no poly blends—or it just won't work.

You might want to start with something simple to test out your color preferences, but a beautiful napkin or tablecloth with embroidered flowers or Victorian detailing can offer gorgeous contrasts when dyed, with the tea soaking differently into the embellished parts.

2. Choose your tea.

+ For a rich, deep brown, go with a strong-brewing black tea such as Mauritius or Cameroon Fannings (mmm . . . delicious! Oh, right—back on topic . . .). These teas will provide a much darker hue and deeper saturation than lighter black teas, such as Sessa or any pekoe- or Assam-based blend.

+ If you're looking for more of a honeyed shade—light and yellowish—go for a rooibos tisane, which produces almost a caramel color.

+ If you're looking for a simple, really subtle green tint, go for a sencha-based tea.

+ If you're looking for a light golden hue—*very* light—use chamomile or peppermint tea if you want to achieve a yellowish green, and white tea if you simply want a light off-white tint.

+ All other tisanes are usually hibiscus-based and will produce a nice pink color (not magenta) that can be hard to darken no matter how long your fabric stews.

3. Find a dyeing vat.

Find a pan or pot or basin that will hold your item (be sure to use something that you don't mind staining) and just enough water to cover the item when soaking.

4. Measure your tea.

Use anywhere from 2 to 30 ounces of loose tea (or 4 to 25 tea bags), keeping in mind the size of the item and the amount of water you're using. Obviously, the more you use, the richer the color and the more the fabric will "drink" in.

As a guideline, about 4 bags of Lipton orange pekoe or 2 ounces of loose afternoon tea will be enough for 2 napkins if you want them to take on a light aged parchment color; whereas 25 of those tea bags or 30-ish ounces of that loose tea will provide the same color for one small tablecloth. We've heard the general rule recommending 4 cups of water for each yard of fabric, or 2 tea bags for each cup of water, but remember that this is all about how your fabric soaks it in and what color you're going for, which is very personal—so perhaps start there, but use your instincts and don't be afraid to experiment!

Note: If you're using loose tea, put it in a tea sock or sac or another kind of strainer so that you can easily remove every tea leaf once you've achieved your desired color.

5. Brew the tea.

Bring the desired amount of water to a boil, take it off the heat, and brew that tea! We recommend 3 minutes or more for black, green, or white teas and 7 minutes or more for herbal (but whenever the color looks dark enough to you, feel free to stop steeping). Keep in mind that the color of the tea is *far* darker than the color of the wet dyed fabric, and once your item is washed and dried, it will be even lighter.

6. Soaking time!

Pour the tea into the basin and add those linens or pillowcases or doilies or anything you feel moved to dye, really, and make sure that they're completely submerged in the tea. Stir every few minutes to ensure that the color is distributing evenly and that no creases are left unsaturated. Let soak about 10 minutes for a lighter color, 30 for medium, and an hour for the deepest saturation.

If you want the fabric to be even darker than that, you'll need to set the color (step 7) and then dye it a second time, but it might be worth it to you! But eventually the fabric just won't get any darker.

7. Set the color.

Wring the fabric out completely; then dry it in the dryer to set the color. (If you're line-drying, damp-iron the fabric first—the heat is what helps to lock in the color.) Now, wash and dry your fabric again to see your actual color result. Important: Do not wash your fabric with commercial detergent, which (crazily enough) is meant to remove tea stains. We recommend Seventh Generation Delicate Care Laundry Detergent or, for an even more fabric-safe option, diluted Dr. Bronner's liquid castile soap.

If you *really* want to go that extra mile to help set the color, you can set up a separate basin of room-temperature salt water and soak your newly tea-dyed item before drying it the first time. Use about 1 tablespoon salt per 1 cup water, and make sure the salt is fully dissolved before you immerse the item.

> Important! Be sure to run a quick cycle on the washer and dryer right after they've held your tea-dyed items, so that you don't run the risk of dyeing your other clothes!

RESOURCES

Alice's Tea Cup carries all the teas and many products featured in this book. If you live in or near New York City—or are visiting from out of town—come see us at one of our three locations:

Alice's Tea Cup, Chapter I
102 West Seventy-third Street
New York, NY 10023

Alice's Tea Cup, Chapter II
156 East Sixty-fourth Street
New York, NY 10065

Alice's Tea Cup, Chapter III
220 East Eighty-first Street
New York, NY 10028

212-734-4TEA (832)

E-mail cookbook@alicesteacup.com with any thoughts or questions you may have for us!

The following teas can be found at alicesteacupgifts.com and at the restaurants:

Black Teas

AFRICAN DEW A rich, full-bodied black tea from Africa. This strong tea is a great coffee substitute.

ALICE'S TEA Our signature blend of Indian black tea and Japanese green tea with vanilla and rose petals. This tea has a dedicated following among our customers.

APRICOT BRANDY Indian black tea with dried apricot pieces. We enjoy this tea so much, we infuse our Curious French Toast with it!

BLACK FRUITS Indian black tea with black currants, blackberries, and blueberries. The perfect dark and fruity tea.

CAMEROON FANNINGS A strong black tea grown at 3,300 feet in an African volcano! Tastes great with a drop of milk.

CHRISTMAS TEA A comforting blend of Indian black tea, hibiscus, raisins, rose hips, almonds, cinnamon, and clove.

CINNAMON APPLE SPICE TEA A spicy and sweet Indian black tea with cinnamon chips and dried apple bits.

EMPRESS BLEND RAJINI A delicate blend of Indian black teas and fragrant rose petals.

GINGER TEA Indian black tea with ginger pieces.

INDIAN CHAI Indian tea spiced with cinnamon, ginger, cardamom, and vanilla. Our barista specially prepares each pot with the perfect amount of milk and honey.

LAPSANG SOUCHONG SUPERIOR A medium whole-leaf tea smoked over rare woods. Strong and flavorful with a campfire-like aroma.

LAVENDER EARL GREY Black tea flavored with bergamot and lavender flowers. A delicate variation on the classic.

MAURITIUS Broken tea leaves with a hint of vanilla. Brewed strong and rich, this tea is a staff favorite and a delight for those new to tea.

MT. EVEREST BREAKFAST A smooth and subtle blend of Assam and Yunnan black teas. Slightly more grassy than most black teas.

CASTLETON ESTATE One of the most prestigious estates in the Darjeeling region of India, Castleton produces this highly prized first flush. Brews to a lovely amber color with a complex muscatel flavor.

CHOCOLATE CHAI Black tea spiced with cinnamon, cardamom, ginger, clove, and vanilla and sweetened with chocolate. A real treat, especially when served with milk and honey.

ORANGE SPICE Indian black tea with orange peel and orange spice flavoring.

ORGANIC GINGER ORANGE PEACH Ginger root, orange peel, and peach flavoring blended in a base of Indian black tea.

PEACH TEA WITH FLOWERS Indian black tea with peach bits and aromatic flowers.

Matt, one of our managers, sneaking a cookie break

PHOENIX DESSERT BLEND A sweet blend of Indian black tea, honey, caramel, and vanilla.

PU ERH Earthy tasting with medicinal properties, pu erh is known to reduce triglycerides and aid stomach ailments. Rising in popularity, this is the perfect after-dinner tea.

RED FRUITS Indian black tea flavored with strawberry, raspberry, red currant, and cherry. A fruity blend with a slightly red infusion.

SESSA A classic Assam with a sweet, tannic, and hearty taste.

ST. MARK Indian black tea blended with Chinese and Tibetan flowers, producing a sweet aroma.

SYMPHONY Indian black tea with strawberries and chocolate.

TRAFALGAR SQUARE Our special mixture of a rich vanilla black tea with refreshing peppermint. A taste reminiscent of peppermint patties!

VANILLA Black tea with vanilla essence.

Green Teas

ENERGITEA Green tea with rooibos, ginseng, linden blossoms, and orange.

GENMAICHA Nutty green tea mixed with corn kernels and toasted rice.

GYOKORO The most sought-after green tea in the world! These leaves are picked once a year in Japan and produce a fresh, grassy cup of tea.

JASMINE MONKEY KING Green tea flavored with white jasmine blossoms. Sourced from the Hunan province of China, it is the oldest known scented tea.

KASHMIRI GREEN CHAI A delicious green tea with ginger, cinnamon, and almond pieces. The rare green tea that takes milk nicely.

MOROCCAN MINT Rich green tea and robust mint leaves. A refreshing, aromatic experience.

ROSE SENCHA Japanese green tea with rose hips and rose petals.

White Teas

DRINK-ME-DETOX Our cleansing blend of pai mu tan, silver needle jasmine, and organic rooibos. This combination of white and red teas provides oodles of antioxidants with a trifling amount of caffeine.

ORGANIC SNOWBUDS A rare white tea from the Fujian province of China. The taste is sweet and savory while the aroma suggests dried flowers and chestnuts.

Keegan sniffing Gyokoro tea, with Miles

PAI MU TAN White tea with a flowery aroma. This tea is detoxifying and rejuvenating.

ROSE TEA MÉLANGE Organic white teas, roses, botanicals, and peppermint. This tea is also fantastic served over ice.

SILVER NEEDLE JASMINE A very delicate and rare white tea blended with jasmine flowers.

Matés

MANGO MATÉ Roasted maté blended with mango.

MATÉ CARNIVAL Roasted maté mixed with cocoa, rooibos, sunflower, cactus, cornflowers, and almonds. A hearty brew!

YERBA MATÉ This unadorned maté showcases the herb's strong signature flavor.

Herbals and Tisanes

APRICOT AND CINNAMON GOLD TISANE An herbal blend of apricot, cinnamon, marigolds, and rooibos.

BERRY BUNCH TISANE A blend of berries and hibiscus that creates a deep red infusion, delicious hot or iced. A great choice for kids.

BIANCA Chamomile flowers mixed with hibiscus and orange peel.

CHRISTMAS BREW A zesty tisane with pineapple, apple, orange, peal, mango, papaya, blackberry, hibiscus, raisins, rose hips, almond, cinnamon, and clove.

EVENING COMFORT An herbal blend of peppermint, lemon peel, and ginger root.

FRENCH VERVAIN An aromatic and refreshing herbal tea with a slight lemon flavor.

HAWAIIAN PARADISE A fruity tisane composed of apple, berries, orange peel, rose hips, hibiscus, and apricot.

HIGH NOON Hibiscus, rose, orange, rose hips, linden, strawberries, and apple.

INSPIRATION Peppermint with rose hips and rose petals; slightly sweet and very refreshing.

MANGO FLIP Mango tisane with pineapple, hibiscus, raisins, and sunflowers. Makes a fantastic iced tea!

ORGANIC GINGER   Pure dried ginger root.

OSMANTHUS FLOWER   A golden yellow flower with a sweet floral aroma. This drink is said to promote beautiful skin.

SPARROW'S SOUL   A smooth herbal blend of French vervain, chamomile, rosebuds, and linden blossoms.

Rooibos

EARL GREY HERBAL   Rooibos flavored with bergamot to create a naturally noncaffeinated variation of Earl Grey.

HERBAL CHAI   Rooibos tea blended with cinnamon, ginger, and anise. Served at Alice's with the perfect amount of milk and honey.

HERBAL CHOCOLATE CHAI   Mini chocolate chips blended into the herbal chai lend a little extra sweetness to this rooibos!

ORGANIC ROOIBOS   Simply unadorned! This organic herb creates a reddish-brown brew with a sweet, earthy flavor.

ROOIBOS ADMIRAL'S CUP   Red bush herb with chocolate and vanilla essences. When served with milk, this makes a healthy alternative to hot chocolate!

ROOIBOS AFRICANA   African violets, cornflowers, and a hint of orange flavoring introduce a subtle citrusy sweetness to the rooibos base.

ROOIBOS BOURBON   Red bush herb flavored with bourbon-vanilla essence; an Alice's favorite and a lovely introduction to rooibos.

ROOIBOS COCONUT VANILLA   Dried coconut flakes and vanilla flavoring sprinkled throughout the red bush herb.

ROOIBOS KIMBERLY   Red bush tea with linden, orange, lemon, and rose petals. A delicious citrus blend.

ROOIBOS PHOENIX   A sweet dessert blend of rooibos, honey, caramel, and vanilla.

ROOIBOS RED FRUITS   Rooibos tea flavored with strawberries, raspberries, red currants, and cherries.

ROOIBOS ST. MARK   Chinese and Tibetan flowers add a subtle sweetness to the earthy rooibos base.

ROOIBOS WEDDING CHAI   Rooibos herb with green cardamom and vanilla. Served with milk and honey.

Ingredients

We recommend the following ingredients because they provide good, consistent results for the home baker and cook.

Amy's Bread golden raisin semolina fennel bread (amysbread.com)

Baker's Semi-Sweet Chocolate

Brach's Star Brites peppermint candy

Cacao Barry Dark "Favorites Mi-Amère" Pistoles (www.cacao-barry.com)

Carnation sweetened condensed milk

Hecker's unbleached all-purpose flour

Hershey's butterscotch chips

Hershey's unsweetened cocoa powder (some of the fancier cocoa powders have a tendency to be dry, so we recommend Hershey's except for our Cocoa Loco, for which we recommend Valrhona cocoa powder)

Mae Ploy sweet chili sauce

Marshmallow Fluff

Medaglia D'Oro instant espresso powder

Muir Glen chopped or crushed canned tomatoes

Nutella hazelnut spread

Rice Krispies cereal

Party Goods

www.alicesteacupgifts.com (and our tea
shops, of course!) for teapots, tea sets,
strainers, drip-catchers, and fairy wings

eBay.com for linens, china, tea stands, cake
stands . . . oh, we love eBay!

Rubyzaar.com for colorful flower lights (fair
trade and made out of hand-dyed leaves!)

Justmorocco.com for Moroccan tea glasses
(we use these as votive holders, but . . .)

Rickys-nyc.com for Mattese glitter

Twosmartcookies.com for great cookie cutter
shapes

Allholidaytreasures.com for beautiful string
lights of unusual colors

Oilclothbytheyard.com for beautiful, colorful
oilcloths for outdoor tables

Plumparty.com for amazing paper supplies,
such as napkins, tablecloths, plates, and
more

Aprons by Gwendolyn Allis,
available at www.gwendolynallis.com

ACKNOWLEDGMENTS

Thanks to: Michael, for encouraging us to bring Alice's Tea Cup to fruition, helping us through the many stages, and *tirelessly* keeping us up and running. Your dedication is unparalleled, and you're the most patient impatient person we know!

Mom and Dad—the best parents in the world—for their unconditional trust, faith, encouragement, love, and support. You taught us to be creative, to trust our instincts, to see things through, to keep our hearts (and eyes and ears) open, and to appreciate the roller coaster we're all on. Yes, we *do* know how lucky we are. (And thanks for teaching us how to stay up past 4:00 A.M. It really comes in handy. Well, actually, not really . . .)

Devan Pierce, for *being* our Alice . . . for a dollar. Your beauty, inside and out, has always astounded us.

Devon and Rena Shah, for inspiration, advice, and the best teas in the world.

Ethel Barber, for the love and encouragement most daughters-in-law are not fortunate enough to receive.

Jodi, David, Hannah, Rachel, and Sam Rubenstein and Ann, Don, Deanne, Adam, Kaja, and Natasha Thomas, for support and love.

Robert, Sheena, Crystal, and Saffire Corzo, for years of love, friendship, support, and hard work!

All our friends—too many to name them all, but who have made us who we are and continue to be, and have supported our dreams and seen us through all the ups and downs with nothing but love. We would both like to thank Adam Lamas, who created our original mural at Chapter III; Melissa Arleth, who painted the Tenniel murals at Chapters I and III and literally cried over spilled milk; Vanessa Daou, who painted the murals at Chapter II; Lauren Berley, who took all of our original photographs!; Christian Nelson, for skillfully announcing to the PR world that Alice's was being born; the Goldsteins; Billy Demeritt; Jeff Hepner, for literally helping us grow; Jessica Grant; Eric Alperin; Junior; Miguel; Kurt Olender, for continuing guidance and friendship; the Pressels, for incredible support and introducing us to "the auction"; Evan Ruster; Don Hurwitz; Joel Saferstien; Lisa Karmen; Oliver Vaquer; Aaron Schindler; Lori Tisch; Jimmy King; Jackie Lann; Mandie Erickson; Suri and Bruce Teitelbaum; Hillary and Arron Schwartz; and Tracy and Enrique, whom we miss and love dearly. Thank you to Mark Nadler, K. T. Sullivan, Joan Scott, Ellen Marks, Celeste Holm and Frank Basile, Rona Roberts and family, the Astrachans, the Kurtzmans, the Colodnes, Fredda Harris and family, Trudy Schlachter, Kelly and Jay Tunney, Janet Davis, La Chanze, the Forstadts and family, Alice Michaels, the Mendelows, the Agins, and Pia Lindstrom.

Lauren would like to thank Mishna Wolff, for being my very best friend through so many ups and downs, and sharing (and preserving) an important history with me; Michelle Esparza, for always listening, never judging, and at times calming me down like no other friend can (and sharing my addiction to Mt. Everest tea!); Raul Esparza, for your friendship and love; Linda Kaufman, for loving Alice's and eating there all the time, and for your amazing and generous heart; John Keegan, for over three years of loyal patronage—I'm so grateful to finally know your sweet self; Elizabeth Freund, for your many years of love, inspiration, friendship, and radiant inner beauty; Anora Wolff, my other little sis; Coke O'Neal, for our new "old" friendship that I cherish deeply; Michael Zampino, for being part of my "inner circle"; Frank Hannah, for your friendship and many wise words over the years; Cyd Levin, for your unwavering belief in me and endless enthusiasm for all that I do; Jason Sasportas, for your incredible patience and understanding about my schedule while we were writing this book; Billy and Clara Hopkins, for your regular father-daughter teas at Alice's and for years of friendship; John Ryan, for years of friendship and a place to lay my head on the West Coast; Yoonah

Shoji, for (literally) the clothes on my back; Micheline Babich, for being an "always friend" and helping me navigate through some tricky times; Michael Bernard Beckwith, for the wisdom, inspiration, and teachings that I carry with me every day; Betsy Landis, you are the big sister I never had, and my gratitude is massive; Michael Eisenberg, I'm glad I'm not dead or in jail for homicide—we have worked through it, and I love you, my brother; Maddan and Finley, for being the lightest, brightest, most beautiful part of my life; and, last, but *most* important, my sweet, always wise beyond her years, awe-inspiring sister—what a journey it's been! You've seen me through the very best and the very worst with your unique brand of selfless, unconditional love. You are my friend, my confidante, my refuge, my rock, and my other half, now and always. . . .

Haley would like to thank Betsy, for one-of-a-kind unconditional love and advice for twenty years and beyond measure; Maria, for unparalleled friendship every hour of every day (there are no words for it . . .); Rachel (dear, amazing Rachel), who has been both an Alice's enthusiast and a Haley enthusiast for twelve years and constantly fills me up with generous love; Ann, who is somewhat new to my life but has improved it immensely and already feels like family; Samantha, who *is* family and has so much to do with the person I am today; Laura, whose strong support and love has fueled me and for whom I am so grateful; Tava, for dear friendship and tremendous support of Alice's; Alanna, the Daous, Margo, Elizabeth, Jenna, Kori, Anne, Tamara, Gloria, Noa, Jen, Megan, Abigail, Karen, Caitlin, Jessica, Lauren, and a ton of amazing people from PS87 and the YMCA, whom I value and appreciate. Special thanks also to Eliza and Brian, whom I love as family and who personally helped Alice's thrive and grow. All these people deserve the moon and stars and everything in between. To my amazing husband, my rock and the best friend ever—I don't know how you do it all, but thank you for doing it again and again and again. To my kids, who make me smile so many times each day: You are my heart. Period. And, finally, to my sister, without whom I have *no* idea who I would be. We've had quite a ride, and it will keep going. Thank you for your massive heart, your praise, your wisdom, your imagination, and your time. You give all of them equally and freely.

Thanks to all the staff and friends involved in the "making" of this cookbook, and to those who lent their beautiful faces to the photos.

Florence Fabricant (who shares our love of Alice herself), Eric Asimov, Robin Raisfeld, Amy Zavatto, Isabel Forgang, and other critics who have said nice things about us over the years.

Carla Glasser, for approaching us about a cookbook and believing it was really going to happen. Thanks to Ben Fink for your incredible talent! And to Cassie Jones, for not only being the most patient, reasonable, and fun editor, but also for trusting our vision.

Thank you to all the staff that has enabled Alice's to grow and thrive beyond our wildest dreams—in particular, Sue McClinton, who might be the best baker on earth; Julie Taras, who has successfully spun her talents into her own delectable dream in Little Giant (and to Darby for introducing us!); Danielle Honzik,

for helping us get to the next level; Jason Munzer, for years of loyalty and creativity; Sara Nash, for helping us create brunch; and all the staff from the early years, including Devan, Crystal, Jessica, Lea, Louise, Veronica, Hudge, Elena, Hannah, Elizabeth, Snezana, Lynn, Natalie, Betsy, Hadas, Rayme, Genevieve, Diana, Clifton, Dante, Brandon, Sammy, Oliver, Isabel, Teo, and Davey. Thank you to Yossy, for creating our party system; Christabel and Betina, for their incredible cakes; and our amazing current managers, Bobby, Julie, Sam, Miles, Matt, Rachel, Katie, Gretchen, Ramiro, and Joe! We know we left some out, but know that we thank *all* of you!

Thanks to all the regulars, especially the little ones! Special thanks to the Rogers family; John Keegan; "the professor"; Claire and Dino; Alice; Claudia; Pam; Daniel Mackenzie; Marilyn; Sheila Grey and "Panini"; cousins Wayne, Aaron, and Max; Shani Glance; Cassie Hurd; Ms. Stella; Daniel and his mom; Nikki; Brenda; Alvia; and Marsha; Lawrence and Fyodor; Paul; Jeff; and Erica; Hue; Stephanie and Hannah;

Andrew; Jessica; Will; Avery and his parents; Mila K.; Steven Stone; Katie and Suri; Lea Michelle; Conan O'Brien; Bernadette Peters; Raul Esparza; Julia Roberts; Bill Macy; Kelly Ripa; John Oliver; Mary-Kate and Ashley Olsen; Natalie; the Buyniaks; William; Sissy S.; the Campbells; Dothan and Fallan; Lance and Moe; Reese and Rye; Lorne M.; and Basil—for drinking nothing but Alice's Earl Grey while on duty in Iraq!

A major thank-you to Mike Brusco, who's been amazing to us; Didi and Andrew Hunter, who offer friendship daily; and Hakim Kamran, who supports us in so many ways.

Everyone who has blogged, Tweeted, Facebooked, or otherwise written in support of Alice's (which is how we met Beth Johnson Nicely and Amanda Kloots-Larsen, otherwise known as "Brownie and Blondie" of www.justdessertsnyc.com).

Last but not least, thanks to Alice Wolfe Reichert, our original Alice—and to her parents, Andrea Marcovicci and Daniel Reichert, for their love, and for their Alice!

We both babysat for Alice when she was younger— one of the reasons we were inspired to reconnect with Alice in Wonderland. We love you, Alice!

INDEX

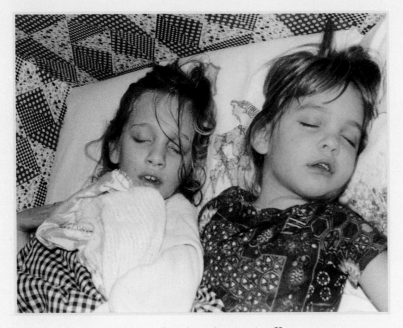

Lauren and Haley, sleeping it off . . .